FOOD ON TAP

FOOD ON TAP

COOKING WITH CRAFT BEER

LORI RICE

THE COUNTRYMAN PRESS

A division of W. W. Norton & Company

Independent Publishers Since 1923

For information about permission to reproduce selections from this book, write to
Permissions, The Countryman Press, 500 Fifth Avenue, New York, NY 10110

For information about special discounts for bulk purchases, please contact
W. W. Norton Special Sales at specialsales@wwnorton.com or 800-233-4830

Manufacturing through Imago
Book design by Anna Reich
Production manager: Devon Zahn

The Countryman Press
www.countrymanpress.com

A division of W. W. Norton & Company, Inc.
500 Fifth Avenue, New York, NY 10110
www.wwnorton.com

978-1-68268-076-6

10 9 8 7 6 5 4 3 2 1

Raise your glass.

To those before us who made beer out of necessity
and to those among us who have turned it into a form of art.

To home and travel. Without them, the beauty of cooking and beer
would never have had the chance to inspire me.

CONTENTS

Make what you eat, eat what you love, and
enjoy beer and food that inspire you.

INTRODUCTION

People who enjoy cooking have a lot in common with craft beer lovers. Both are inspired by new food and drink experiences. The reward of discovering an enjoyable food or drink is well worth the small risk of trying it and not liking it. We smell, analyze, bite or sip, compare it to funny things like grass and ocean breezes, and then bite and sip again.

I expect this is how my love of fresh, simple food evolved into an equal fondness for well-crafted beer. They each have humble beginnings that, with the right touch, can be turned into things so appetizing that we struggle for the words to describe them.

These commonalities are why beer not only works with food, beer works in food. It's a true joy any time we get to have both.

If you haven't considered using your favorite beers in the foods you cook, this book provides you many opportunities to broaden your horizons beyond the realm of chocolate stout cake and beer can chicken. Beer can truly step up your game in the kitchen, and it does so in unexpected ways. The grassy, floral hops in an IPA adds a citrus punch to salad dressings. A fruity, pucker-inducing sour beer makes one tasty strawberry muffin. Beer can be used in recipes for any meal (see the brunch chapter!) and in any course of a meal.

This book is meant to take two works of art and combine their best qualities to make something unforgettable. Beer education and cooking know-how can sometimes feel overwhelming, but if you persist your results in the kitchen will surprise you. Combine them and it's a recipe for pure fun. So kindly ask any undeserved lingering snobbery that surrounds craft beer and fine food to step out for a while, or better yet, for good. *Food on Tap* is an accessible guide for cooking with craft beer that I hope will spark a creative curiosity to keep you hopping from the brewery back to the kitchen.

Chapter I

COOKING AND BAKING WITH BEER

I like to think of cooking and baking as an ideal marriage between art and science. The partnership has its challenges, but the relationship is always worth it in the end. The same analogy can be used for craft beer: it's an artisanal product that has a foundation in science. When you bring beer into the art of cooking you pull even more science into the mix, which sometimes complicates the relationship. But once you know some basic rules and combine that knowledge with your understanding of beer styles, cooking with beer will come naturally. You'll soon gain the confidence to do some experimenting of your own.

TIPS FOR SUCCESSFUL COOKING AND BAKING WITH BEER

I've learned a few things over the years by using more and more beers and beer styles in my recipes. You may find the following observations to be helpful guides for how you approach things in your own kitchen.

Relax, it's hard to mess up. Beer is a pretty resilient ingredient. Yes, there is a thing or two you can do that will ruin a bottle, and we'll cover those. But overall, while preparing a dish I find that when I add the beer, what beer I add, and the ideal beer temperature is surprisingly flexible. So relax. If you make a mistake with a recipe, there is a good chance you will still have success in the end.

You can use chilled beer (sometimes). One tricky thing about cooking with beer is whether you should use room temperature beer or if it's okay to grab a bottle from the fridge. This is especially tricky if a recipe uses just a few ounces. I expect, like me, you'd prefer to drink the rest of that freshly opened beer instead of allowing the entire bottle to get to room temperature and go flat.

Let's start with room temperature beer. In general, it will work with all recipes. It's especially important to use room temperature beer in bread and pastry recipes that use yeast or that need to rise. The yeast in the dough and any yeast active in the beer need a warm, cozy environment to do their thing. Avoid chilled beer for these recipes.

Otherwise, chilled beer gives successful results. Grab the beer out of the fridge when you get started, though, so it's chilled and not ice-cold. Also remember that a chilled beer may influence cooking times. For example, if you pour a chilled beer into a soup or stew at the final step, it will take extra time for it to heat back up to serving temperature.

Less fizz is best, but the foam won't cause you to fail. It's usually best to pour your beer into the measuring cup and let the head settle before adding it to your recipe. This helps prevent excess foaming and spills that can happen when it hits the other ingredients. That being said, you don't want the beer to be completely flat, as in, it sat open in the fridge for a few days. That carbonation has a leavening role in many recipes, so you need to give the fizz just enough time to calm down before you use it. This isn't the case for every single recipe, but for the sake of consistency, measure the beer five minutes or so before you need it. If you forget, don't panic. You can add it from the bottle, just be aware that you might need to lower the temperature of the burner for a minute to prevent the beer from foaming over the side of the saucepan.

Use flavor as your guide. Before you set out to use beer in a recipe, drink it. Note its aroma, its initial flavors, and its lingering impression on your tongue. If it brings a food to mind, chances are it would be a nice beer to use in making it. This is why I love using chile beers in corn bread and salsa, and pale ales in salad dressings. You might find a smoked porter to be a better match for your corn bread and an IPA for your dressing. Simply put, experiment!

Break the rules. If you knew me well, you would gasp at the sight of this one in my list. I'm not one for the saying, "Rules were made to be broken"—except when it comes to the rules regarding cooking and baking with beer. Some of those rules, for example, are that a stout is the best fit for a chocolate cake, and hoppy beers should be avoided because they turn bitter.

I can give you a list of five beers that work as well or better in a chocolate cake than a stout. Yes, a hoppy IPA with IBUs of 75 may turn bitter when it's boiled or baked at high heat, but since when has well-balanced bitterness in good food been a bad thing? It's okay to nudge the gate open and try something new. (By the way, IBUs stands for International Bitterness Units. If you happen to be unfamiliar with the measure, don't worry. We discuss it further in chapter 2.)

Sometimes less beer is better. This book gives you options to cook with beer for most meals and every course of the meal. That doesn't mean I would encourage you to use beer in every dish on the table. When used in food, beer is complex and direct. What tastes excellent at the start of a meal might wear out your taste buds by the end. Pick and choose beer-infused dishes to blend with and complement other foods. On the same note, some of these recipes pair wonderfully with beer to sip while you eat. I've noted my suggestions throughout the book. Other recipes don't pair as successfully. For example, dishes like the Roasted Winter Squash Soup with Stout Brown Sugar Bacon (page 79) and the American Wheat and White Bean Stew (page 84) are deliciously beer-heavy. To pair them with more beer may overpower the palate.

Eat it the same day for the most appetizing experience. Beer isn't always the best ingredient for make-ahead meals. Once it rests for a day or two in the fridge the beer can overpower baked goods and soups. They can begin to taste overly malty and sometimes bitter. There are a few exceptions. For example, the Chile Beer Tomatillo Salsa (page 60) improves after the flavors marry for a day, but in my experience this is rare. I've noted when recipes can be made ahead or how long a recipe can be kept fresh (it's usually 3 days, max). This doesn't necessarily mean that the food is spoiled after this amount of time, but it does mean that the taste becomes less than optimal. For the most part, you can assume your beer dishes are best eaten right after they are prepared.

THE ROLE OF BEER AND MISTAKES TO AVOID

I like to think that mistakes are just new recipes waiting to happen. But if you've spent enough time in the kitchen, then you know that epic fails sometimes do happen. I say this not to scare you but to encourage you to broaden your knowledge of how beer performs as an ingredient and not just how it's brewed and tastes as a beverage.

Just like the flour, baking soda, or olive oil in a recipe, beer has specific qualities that dictate how it will behave. Beer is acidic and acts like other acidic recipe ingredients. Beer can curdle delicate ingredients like milk. A higher fat content like that in whole milk or half-and-half versus skim milk helps offset curdling. The yeast in beer also has leavening abilities. But this doesn't always mean that beer alone can produce the same leavening results as other ingredients, such as dry active yeast. For most recipes in this book, the other ingredients are adjusted so that the beer can bring its positive qualities to the final dish.

The pleasant bitterness in beer, of course, comes from hops. More specifically it comes from the alpha acids, which are chemical compounds in the hops. When beer is boiled, or exposed to high heat for an extended period of time, that bitterness intensifies. It can become bitter to an unpalatable level if certain precautions are not practiced.

Sugar balances bitterness. For this reason, you'll find that sugar is added before reducing a beer, such as in the Holiday Ale Cut-Out Cookies (page 161). While sugar is not always the solution, there are times when you can use it to rescue a recipe result that is a little too bitter for your preferences. For example, adding a little more sugar, or a sweet ingredient like orange juice, to a salad dressing can cut some bitterness.

It is important to pay attention to the beer suggested in the recipe and consider its level of bitterness. I do believe in experimenting, but when selecting alternative beers it's often best to stay within a similar level of bitterness and hop profile if a recipe calls for boiling or cooking at high heat. For instance, if a session IPA is listed in a recipe, a double (or imperial) IPA may be too high in alcohol and bitterness to be used as a substitute. Burner control is an important skill to develop when cooking with beer. Although everyone's stovetop is a little different, simmer always means simmer. If you add beer to a soup that needs to simmer, but you turn up the heat and walk away, returning to find it at a boil, you may have just ruined dinner. If it turned bitter, some sugar might balance it. But it's best to avoid the situation altogether and stay attentive in the kitchen. Maybe save the second pint to drink with your meal and not while cooking it.

TIPS FOR INGREDIENTS BEYOND BEER

In the kitchen, we all have ingredients that we turn to most often and ways of doing things that work best for us. You'll notice some trends along those lines throughout the book, so I thought it would be best to outline a few of those things before you get started. I'm a believer that higher quality, fresh ingredients give the best end result. That applies to all the things mentioned here.

Fine sea salt: The topic of salt tends to be a bone of contention among people who spend a significant amount of time in the kitchen. A few years ago I started using fine ground sea salt in all my cooking and baking, and I haven't looked back. I like its mild level of intensity. Personally, I prefer it over kosher salt. If you use a different type of salt, keep in mind that intensities vary. Add a little at a time, and taste as you go.

Shredded cheese: There's no substitute for shredding your own cheese. That's why you will find cheese listed in ounces in this book. For me, it's the only option when I'm using it in recipes where it's melted, such as the Three Cheese IPA Soup Shooters (page 59). Some preshredded cheeses have other ingredients added to keep them from clumping, and these can influence how smoothly they melt. Weigh your block first and then shred. I promise, it takes only five extra minutes, tops. If it's a large amount, a food processor with a grater blade is especially helpful.

Whole-fat dairy: A higher fat content can offset some curdling effects an acidic beer might bring to a recipe. All the recipes in this book use full-fat dairy, including the cheese. Plus, it simply tastes better and is more satisfying.

HELPFUL KITCHEN TOOLS

When I look at a bottle of beer I see it in ounces: 12 ounces, 22 ounces, etc. It doesn't automatically translate to 1½ cups in my head. So while recipes in this book rely on standard U.S. measurements such as a cup and a tablespoon, you'll find that the beer measurements are in ounces. That way you know at a quick glance if you need a full bottle of beer, half of a beer, or another amount. Nonetheless, a measuring cup with the fluid ounces clearly marked is an essential tool for cooking with beer.

A kitchen scale will help you weigh those blocks of cheese and a few other ingredients here and there. And if you don't already own a candy thermometer, I highly suggest you obtain one. You'll need it for the Milk Stout Caramel Tart (page 172). Alcohol influences the boiling temperature of caramel, and it is nearly impossible to use a simple timing method. A candy thermometer will ensure the caramel in the recipe comes to the right temperature for the best filling.

Chapter 2

BEER STYLES IN THIS BOOK

Given all the innovative styles of craft beer, I find that all it takes to be filled with cooking inspiration is an afternoon of beer tasting. A sip of a well-crafted barleywine with notes of sweet raisin sends my thoughts straight to an oatmeal raisin cookie. Spiced citrus flavors of a witbier linger on my tongue and stimulate visions of biscuits and scones. These are the beers you know and love. Once you consider their flavors with food in mind, you may no longer be able to sip your way through a tasting flight without mentally adapting all of your favorite recipes.

If you are ready to cook with beer, it's probably a safe bet that you've tried your fair share of brews. Meaning, you are aware of the many styles and flavor profiles available. That's why I won't go into too much detail about what beer is, and why I won't discuss every beer style out there. Instead, I focus on a selection of beers, examine why these beers work with food, and provide substitutes when they are appropriate.

The recipes in this book were developed with accessibility in mind. You should have no problem getting your hands on any of the beer styles used in these recipes if you have at least one craft brewery, bottle shop, or craft-stocked supermarket nearby. If you live in a craft beer mecca, there is plenty of opportunity for you to take advantage of that variety. You can walk the straight and narrow with a stout, pale ale, or IPA, but I've also noted where you might lean toward a specialty coffee and vanilla infused stout, pine or herb prominent pale ale, or a tangerine and grapefruit IPA.

Before we get cooking, let's discuss a couple of beer terms that you might already be familiar with: ABV and IBUs. Understanding them is important because of how they influence taste and recipe use.

Alcohol by Volume, or ABV, is listed as a percentage. Since yeast converts sugar into alcohol during fermentation, ABV depends on the activity of the yeast. This leads to big differences among beer styles as well as aging times and methods. Don't be fooled by things like color to determine ABV. Look instead at style and brewing method. A holiday porter ABV can hover around 5.5 percent and have a dark brown color that is similar to a bourbon barrel–aged beer that tips the scale at 12 percent.

Alcohol matters in cooking and baking because it can determine the sharpness of flavor. For example, when using beer in soups and stews a full bottle of a low-alcohol beer may be added for a balanced flavor. Add the same amount of a high-alcohol beer and the sharp taste may be too overwhelming to bear. I find higher-alcohol beers are better for splashes of flavor, or for macerating and marinating.

International Bitterness Units, or IBUs, is a measure of a beer's bitterness. It's typically measured on a scale of 0 to 100, although some specialty beers can exceed 100. A higher number indicates a more bitter beer. Bitterness is most strongly related to hop content, but because bitterness can be controlled by a balance of hops and malt, not every beer is bitter simply because it contains hops. Beer styles typically reflect IBUs, but there are exceptions as brewers continue to innovate. IPAs usually have IBUs of 50 to 75, and are often regarded as the most bitter style of beers. Brewers have been known to boost the hop content of beers that are typically lower on the IBU scale, like saisons and wheat beers, which can increase the bitterness.

The IBU level plays a role in how a beer will taste in a final dish and steers what cooking methods and foods are the best fit for the beer. The goal is to play on all flavor attributes of the beer style and not to allow bitterness to take over where it isn't wanted. While you may not be able to find the IBUs of a beer every time, knowing the style is at least a starting point for understanding its level of bitterness.

Now, we'll take a look at the beers used as ingredients in this book. I've made my suggestions for what tastes lend themselves to certain foods. Of course, you may envision other culinary pairings to experiment with. I've listed the typical ABVs and IBUs of the styles, but keep in mind that these are approximations based on my own brewery hopping and information from the Cicerone Certification Program, which is an organization that certifies and educates beer professionals. There are definitely outliers on the market within a specific style, and the variations in ABV and IBU depend on how the beer is brewed and aged.

Note that in the listings that follow, I provide substitutes that are equally delicious in case the beer is seasonal or you simply can't find it. The substitutes aren't always an exact match for the beer in terms of drinking, but they will produce tasty results in the types of foods suggested for the beer. Some of the substitutes aren't used in the recipes in this book, but I present them here so that you may find a beer that will give you an equally enjoyable result in the kitchen.

At the end of each recipe you will also find alternative beers to consider. This is to help you with ingredient shopping. I've included both widely distributed beers and more regional options. I also encourage you to use beer shopping as an excuse to talk with local brewers and bottle shop owners so that you can learn about all of the varieties available. Chances are you'll come home with some great craft bottles or a growler fill.

Amber Ale. Also called a red ale, this beer has a hop bitterness that is balanced by malt sometimes emitting caramel and toffee notes. It goes well in savory starters and sides, especially those with caramelized onions. It is also a good fit for sweets like chocolate.

ABV: 4.5 to 6.5 percent; IBUs: 25 to 40

Substitute: Brown Ale, Brown Porter

Barleywine. American barleywines are rich and syrupy with deep fruity notes like raisin. They can also have a fair amount of hoppiness. They add a richness to beef stews and a fruity sweetness to desserts.

ABV: 8 to 12; IBUs: 50 to 100

Substitute: Barrel-Aged Beer

Barrel-Aged. Barrel aging can be applied to any style of beer. Brewers make use of bourbon, tequila, rum, and wine barrels (to name a few) for aging beer. The beer then takes on qualities of that spirit or wine. Bourbon barrel–aged brown ales and stouts are my favorite to use because they go so well with desserts. These beers tend to be high in alcohol, so I use them as more of a flavoring as you would vanilla.

ABV: 8 to 12 percent; IBUs: dependent on the beer style being aged

Substitute: For desserts, choose similar beer styles aged in rum or brandy barrels

Belgian Strong Golden Ale. Floral, fruity, crisp, and clean, the Belgian strong golden ale can be high in alcohol but lower in hop bitterness. I use it in both savory and sweet tart and pie crusts. A splash can also brighten a savory or sweet filling.

ABV: 7.5 to 10.5 percent; IBUs: 20 to 35

Substitute: Belgian Blonde Ale

Blonde Ale. Light and biscuity, American blonde ales complement bread doughs and add a savory component to sauces. You can often find honey blonde ales that have an added touch of sweetness.

ABV: 3.5 to 5.5 percent; IBUs: 15 to 30

Substitute: American Wheat, Cream Ale

Brown Ale. The American brown ale has toasted notes that hint at caramel and sometimes chocolate. Its low hop bitterness makes it ideal for casseroles and beans with longer baking times.

ABV: 4 to 6.2 percent; IBUs: 20 to 40

Substitute: English Brown Ale, Amber Ale

California Common. The most notable characteristic about the common is the use of a historic brewing method that uses a lager yeast at the warmer temperatures associated with ales. It produces a malty amber brew with moderate bitterness that works well in bread doughs.

ABV: 4.5 to 5.5 percent; IBUs: 30 to 45

Substitute: Blonde Ale, Helles

Cream Ale. Cream ales have malty, cornlike notes and low bitterness. You'll find variations with all sorts of ingredients such as coffee, vanilla, fruits, and honey to create a light, crisp beer that subtly hints at dessert. Cream ales make great additions to cakes and cupcakes.

ABV: 4 to 5.5 percent; IBUs: 15 to 20

Substitute: Light Lager

Fruit and Chile Beer. The beers in this category differ from other fruity beers like lambics and sours because these don't use wild yeast. They are ales and lagers infused with fruits such as blackberries or chilies such as jalapeños. They carry a mild touch of their sweet and spicy characteristics with them into the final dish. Fruit beers can be used in everything from meat glazes to cakes and pies. Chile beers add a spicy touch to breads and salsas.

ABV: 4.5 to 9 percent; IBUs: dependent on type of beer infused

Substitute: Lambic, Saison

Helles. A historic German beer style, the helles has malty, breadlike notes that lend well to pretzel doughs and to meats such as sausage.

ABV: 4.5 to 5.5 percent; IBUs: 15 to 25

Substitute: German-Style Pilsner

Holiday Beer. This group includes pumpkin ales and winter warmers—beers that mimic the holidays through malty flavors, seasonal produce, or the use of spices like cinnamon and nutmeg. As expected, they are ideal for holiday desserts, but they can add a pleasant taste to beans and roasted meats any time of the year.

ABV: 5.5 to 8 percent; IBUs: 20 to 45

Substitute: Brown Ale, Amber Ale, Fruit Beer, Hefeweizen

India Pale Ale and Double India Pale Ale. The American India pale ale (IPA) is full of hoppy bitterness that often presents itself in citrus flavors and piney notes. I use IPA in cheese sauces, dressings, and citrus-infused cakes. The double India pale ale (DIPA), or imperial IPA, is higher in alcohol and often hoppier than a standard IPA. It's best for soaking or marinating fruits for desserts, and can also work as a marinade for meat.

ABV: 5.5 to 12 percent; IBUs: 40 to 100

Substitute: Pale Ale, English IPA

Lambic. Brewed with wild yeast, lambic is a fruity beer that can be tart and acidic. It plays well with savory dishes using beef and bison. With little to no bitterness, it is also good for use in desserts. Many lambics made in the United States lean toward the sour, so for more sweetness when using it with savory meats, don't be afraid to explore the Belgian import section of your favorite bottle shop.

ABV: 3 to 8 percent; IBUs: 0 to 10

Substitute: Fruit Beer, Sour Beer

Maibock. This German spring beer has a malty sweetness with a touch of toffee that's balanced by a little hoppy bitterness. It's sweet enough to use in pancakes but also goes well with the earthiness of mushrooms and goat cheese.

ABV: 6 to 7.5 percent; IBUs: 20 to 35

Substitute: Amber Ale

Märzen. Often labeled as Oktoberfest, the German märzen has characteristics of toasted, malty bread. Although it's not too sweet, it can have caramel notes. It works well in everything from stews to sweet rolls.

ABV: 4.5 to 6 percent; IBUs: 20 to 30

Substitute: Amber Ale, Brown Ale

Mexican Lager. Mexican lagers from U.S. craft brewers often fall into the category of American pale lagers, but with a nod to historic Mexican brewing methods using corn, or maize, and Vienna malts. The crisp sweetness works well in any type of Mexican-inspired dish.

ABV: 4 to 6 percent; IBUs: 5 to 20

Substitute: Vienna-Style Lager, Chile Beer

Pale Ale. American pale ales have crisp flavors of citrus and can be quite hoppy. English pale ales are also fruity and hoppy but maintain more malty notes with hints of butter that balance the bitterness. Pale ales are a good match for rich and buttery sauces or dressings as well as pasta sauces.

ABV: 3.5 to 7 percent; IBUs: 30 to 45

Substitute: India Pale Ale

Pilsner. A pilsner is bright, crisp, and refreshing. Czech-style pilsners have a stronger maltiness, while the German style has a slight floral hoppiness. I like to use pilsner in batters and breading for meats, and for quick pickling.

ABV: 4 to 5.5 percent; IBUs: 25 to 45

Substitute: Helles, Kölsch

Porter. History has it that stouts evolved from the porter, but in cooking they deserve to be recognized as two distinct beers. Porters exhibit fewer of the heavily roasted coffee notes of a stout, and more of a chocolaty, malty flavor with less bitterness. Many brewers make porters to mimic desserts by infusing vanilla, chocolate, or coconut. I like to use standard brown and robust porters in savory, earthy dishes such as wild rice. Smoked porters go well in dips and savory quick breads. Dessert porters are best for cakes and pies.

ABV: 4 to 6.5 percent; IBUs: 20 to 50

Substitute: Stout, English Brown Ale

Saison. Sometimes called farmhouse ales, saisons have a peppery quality that goes well with savory soups but also adds a level of interest to desserts such as brownies.

ABV: 5 to 7 percent; IBUs: 20 to 35

Substitute: Belgian Pale Ale

Session Beer. A session beer contains no more than 5 percent ABV. Session can apply to any style of beer but is common with IPAs. I find that session IPAs have a lower risk of turning bitter in baked goods, such as cakes, but still offer the citrus bite.

ABV: 5 percent or lower; IBUs: depends on the style of beer

Substitute: India Pale Ale, or the standard version of the session style

Scottish Ale. A beer that is rich with caramel notes and sometimes a hint of smokiness, I like Scottish ale best in buttery cookies and dessert bars. It is similar to the Scotch ale, but the latter is higher in alcohol.

AVB: 3 to 7 percent; IBUs: 10 to 30

Substitute: Amber Ale, Scotch Ale

Sour Beer. Often referred to as American Wild Ales. Like the lambic, sour beers use wild yeast for fermentation, but the final brew reaches a level of tartness that sets this style apart. Many sour beers are brewed with fruit, and I like to use them as marinades for fruits or nuts before incorporating them into muffins and cakes.

ABV: 5 to 10 percent; IBUs: 0 to 25 (often not reported)

Substitute: Lambic, Gueuze, Gose

Stout and Milk Stout. Stouts are similar to porters but have more bitter coffee notes and tend to be higher in alcohol. Irish stout has the lowest alcohol but holds true to the burnt coffee notes. American stouts sometimes have a stronger hop bitterness. Milk stouts, or sweet stouts, are sweet and creamy due to the addition of lactose (milk sugar) during brewing. These beers are often infused with ingredients like vanilla and coconut. American and Irish stouts are ideal for slow-cooked meats and glazes. Spiced and milk stouts create wonderful bars, candies, and cookies.

ABV: 4 to 7 percent; IBUs: 20 to 75

Substitute: Porter

Wheat Beer. My favorite wheat beers are German hefeweizens because they have strong flavors of banana and clove. American wheats are a little hoppier and lack the banana and clove notes. Wheat beers add a balanced sweetness to stews and to condiments like barbecue sauce and dressings.

ABV: 4 to 5.5 percent; IBUs: 8 to 30

Substitute: Witbier

Witbier. With notes of orange peel and peppery spices such as coriander, the Belgian-style witbier is crisp, refreshing, and low in bitterness. I like to use it in breakfast foods such as biscuits, and in salad dressings.

ABV: 4.5 to 5.5 percent; IBUs: 10 to 20

Substitutes: American Wheat, German-Style Hefeweizen

Chapter 3

FOR BRUNCH

My favorite eating occasion is the melting pot of a meal that we affectionately call brunch. With brunch, there is no judgment. You can choose a quiche, a soup, or a pancake, and no one will think a thing of it. It's also perfectly okay to have your meal with an alcoholic beverage, despite that it is well before noon. Brunch provides a golden opportunity to incorporate craft beer into cooking. It makes breads and biscuits fluffy, caramel rolls rich and buttery, and soups smooth and tangy. Whether you are in the mood for savory or sweet, craft beer is a versatile ingredient to satisfy your brunch needs.

Giant Witbier Biscuit Egg Sandwiches

WITBIER OR WHITE ALE

The best beer swap you can make for breakfast is to trade the dairy in home-made biscuits for a crisp witbier. Beer helps the biscuits bake up light and fluffy, but with edges that have a buttery crunch. These big biscuits have over-easy eggs tucked inside with sharp Cheddar and a few sprigs of arugula for a pop of green and a peppery bite.

SERVES 3

BISCUITS

2 cups unbleached all-purpose flour
2 teaspoons baking powder
½ teaspoon fine sea salt
3 scallions, white and green
    portions sliced
½ cup (1 stick) cold unsalted butter,
    cubed, plus 1 tablespoon, melted
6 ounces witbier

EGGS

3 slices sharp Cheddar
6 eggs, cooked over easy (or to your
    preference)
1 cup arugula

Preheat the oven to 425°F.

Stir together the flour, baking powder, salt, and scallions in a medium bowl. Add the butter. Use a pastry blender or two knives to work the dough until the butter is evenly distributed in pea-sized pieces. Stir in the beer and form the dough into a ball.

Split the dough into two equal portions. Flatten each portion to 2½ inch thickness. Cut each with a 4-inch circle biscuit cutter. Roll the remaining scraps to just beyond a 4-inch circle and cut with the biscuit cutter. Place all 3 biscuits on an ungreased baking sheet or a baking sheet covered in a silicone mat. Bake for 20 minutes, until golden brown and baked through the center.

Let cool for 2 to 3 minutes. While still warm, split each biscuit in half. Place a slice of cheese on the bottom portion, add two eggs, and some of the arugula. Add the top portion of the biscuit and serve.

Note: This recipe makes three large egg sandwiches. It can be modified to make more biscuits by using a 2- to 3-inch cutter. For smaller biscuits, be sure to adjust the baking time. It will likely decrease to 12 to 15 minutes.

Beers to consider: Allagash Brewing Company Allagash White, Lagunitas Brewing Company Stoopid Wit, Boston Beer Company Samuel Adams White Ale

Sausage-Crusted Helles and Kale Quiche

HELLES

In this hearty brunch recipe, a pie pan is lined with sausage and then filled with a beer-infused mix of eggs and kale. It's light on the brew, but just the touch of helles gives both the sausage and the eggs a malty yet crisp pop. Pair it with the rest of the helles when serving.

SERVES 6 TO 8

CRUST
½ pound uncooked pork sausage
¼ cup panko bread crumbs
½ ounce helles, divided

FILLING
1 tablespoon extra virgin olive oil
½ bunch of kale, finely chopped
    (about 2 cups)
2 garlic cloves, minced
2½ ounces helles
½ teaspoon fine ground sea salt,
    divided
3 ounces sharp Cheddar, shredded
6 large eggs
1 tablespoon unbleached all-
    purpose flour

Preheat the oven to 350°F.

For the crust, combine the sausage, panko bread crumbs, and ½ ounce of helles in a medium bowl. Place the sausage mixture in a 9-inch pie pan and press into the bottom and sides to create a crust. Bake for 5 minutes, until the sausage just begins to turn from pink to gray over the top.

For the filling, heat the olive oil in a medium skillet over medium-high heat. Add the kale and cook until its color brightens, about 1 minute. Add the garlic and 2 ounces of the helles. Cook until most of the beer evaporates, about 2 minutes. Season with ¼ teaspoon of the salt.

Spread the kale in a single layer over the sausage in the pie pan. Sprinkle the Cheddar over the kale.

Beat the eggs with a whisk in a medium bowl. Whisk in the flour and then the remaining ½ ounce of beer and ¼ teaspoon of salt.

Place the pie pan on a baking sheet to prevent any spills. Pour the eggs into the pie pan over the sausage and kale. Bake for 40 minutes, until the top of the quiche begins to brown and the center is firm. Remove from the oven and let sit for 5 minutes. Cut into 6 to 8 pieces and serve. The quiche will keep in an airtight container in the refrigerator for up to 2 days.

Beers to consider: Victory Brewing Company Victory Helles Lager, Maui Brewing Company Bikini Blonde Lager, Hangar 24 Craft Brewery Wheels Up Helles Lager

Blonde Buns
with Ham and Cheese

BLONDE ALE

My husband and I lived in Brazil for three years, and during that time I tried to experience every aspect of the bakery and café culture there. If I wasn't having a coffee or a juice, I was swinging by to pick up bread for dinner. These bakeries were where I encountered the best version of a ham and cheese sandwich: salty meat and pungent cheese rolled tightly into a tender white roll. When I set out to make my own version, I added blonde ale. Crisp and malty, this beer provides leavening without too much hoppiness to compete with the strong flavors of the meat and cheese tucked inside.

MAKES 12 BUNS

DOUGH

½ cup whole milk

2 tablespoons unsalted butter

1 tablespoon granulated sugar

1 teaspoon dry active yeast

3¼ cups unbleached all-purpose flour

4 ounces blonde ale, room temperature

2 large eggs

1 teaspoon fine sea salt

Extra virgin olive oil, to coat bowl

FILLING

2 ounces sliced deli ham, cut into 12 pieces

2 ounces sliced provolone or Swiss cheese, cut into 12 pieces

1 tablespoon water, room temperature

Warm the milk and the butter in a medium saucepan over medium heat until the butter melts. Transfer the liquid to a heat-safe bowl and cool to 110 to 115°F. Stir in the sugar and yeast. Let sit. Allow the yeast to bloom, about 5 minutes.

Add the flour to the bowl of an electric mixer fitted with a dough hook. Pour in the bloomed yeast. Turn the mixer to medium. Pour in the beer. Continue to mix on medium for 1 minute. Scrape the sides of the bowl as needed. Add one egg and mix until combined. Add the salt.

As the dough mixes, it should begin to form a ball in the middle of the bowl. It should hold its shape and be only slightly sticky. If it seems too dry or too sticky, add a teaspoon of water or a sprinkle of flour as needed for you to handle it during kneading. Turn the dough out onto a floured surface and knead for 5 minutes, until the dough is smooth and elastic. Form the dough into a ball.

Coat a large bowl with olive oil and place the dough in the bowl. Cover with a clean dish towel and let sit in a draft-free place until it doubles in size, about 1 hour.

Punch down the dough and knead it back into a ball. Cut the dough into 12 equal pieces. Roll each piece of dough into a circle, about 4 inches in diameter. Place a piece of ham and cheese in the center of the circle. Tuck in the sides of the circle and roll the dough up tightly to seal in the

continued

ham and cheese. Place the buns seam side down on a baking sheet covered with parchment paper or a silicone baking mat.

Let rise for 15 minutes.

Preheat the oven to 400°F.

In a small bowl, whisk together the remaining egg with the 1 tablespoon of water. Generously brush the outside of each bun with egg wash. Bake for 15 minutes, until the buns are browned on the outside and the bread is baked through. Store the buns in an airtight container in the refrigerator for up to 3 days.

Beers to consider: Any blonde ale is ideal, even one with honey or fruit notes. Try Firestone Walker Brewing Company 805 Blonde Ale, Ska Brewing Company True Blonde Ale, Kona Brewing Company Big Wave Golden Ale

Tomato Blue Cheese Tarts

with Belgian Golden Ale Crust

BELGIAN GOLDEN ALE

These tarts are hands-down my favorite brunch food. The combination of ingredients from tomatoes to honey provides a perfect balance for the taste buds. A little golden ale in the crust and a dash with the filling gives these tarts even deeper flavor. They pair nicely with a golden ale, but the rich cheese also makes a good match for a crisp pilsner.

MAKES 6 TARTS

CRUST

1 cup unbleached all-purpose flour
1 teaspoon granulated sugar
½ teaspoon fine sea salt
½ cup (1 stick) cold unsalted butter, cubed
2 ounces Belgian strong golden ale

FILLING

1 tablespoon extra virgin olive oil
2 tablespoons finely chopped yellow onion
1 pint cherry tomatoes
3 tablespoons chopped raw walnuts
1 ounce Belgian strong golden ale
1 teaspoon honey
½ teaspoon fine sea salt
¼ teaspoon ground black pepper
2 ounces blue cheese, crumbled

Note: The dough for the crust will need to rest in the refrigerator for 30 minutes, so plan accordingly with this one.

To make the crust, place the flour, sugar, and salt in the bowl of a food processor. Add the cubed butter. Pulse for 5- to 10-second intervals, until the butter is evenly distributed in pea-sized pieces. Pour in the beer, pulse for about 30 more seconds, until the dough comes together into a ball. Remove the dough, flatten it slightly into a disk, and wrap it in plastic wrap. Let it rest in the refrigerator for 30 minutes.

For the filling, heat the olive oil in a medium skillet over medium-high heat. Add the onion and cook until it begins to soften, about 2 minutes. Add the cherry tomatoes and cook until most of them begin to burst, about 7 minutes.

Remove the skillet from the heat and stir in the walnuts, beer, honey, salt, and pepper.

Preheat the oven to 400°F.

Roll the crust dough to about ¼-inch thickness on a lightly floured surface. Cut it into six 3½-inch circles. Place each circle into the well of a 6-well jumbo muffin tin. Gently press and spread the dough until it extends three-quarters of the way up the side of each muffin cup.

continued

Spoon an equal amount of the filling into each tart crust. Sprinkle the tarts with crumbled blue cheese.

Bake for 20 to 25 minutes, until the cheese is bubbling and the edges of the crust are golden brown. Let the tarts cool in the pan for at least 5 minutes. Run a butter knife around the edges of each tart and lift them out of the pan. Transfer to a cooling rack to cool completely before serving. These are best served the same day, but they can be kept up to 1 day in an airtight container in the refrigerator. Warm before serving.

Beers to consider: North Coast Brewing Company PranQster, AleSmith Brewing Company Horny Devil, Goose Island Beer Company Matilda

Summer Saison Tomato Bisque

with Black Pepper Croutons

Traditionally bisques were made with blended shellfish, but today the name more accurately designates a soup with some amount of creaminess. This tomato bisque fits the latter description. Peppery saison adds complexity to the sweet tomato. The beer is added toward the end so it stands up well to the other ingredients in the soup. Stick with classic saisons instead of those that have been dry-hopped or barrel aged.

SERVES 4

BISQUE

3 tablespoons unsalted butter
½ large yellow onion, finely chopped (about ¾ cup)
2 garlic cloves, minced
3 tablespoons unbleached all-purpose flour
4 cups low-sodium chicken stock or broth
2 cups tomato sauce
1 tablespoon granulated sugar
4 ounces saison or farmhouse ale
1 to 1½ teaspoons fine sea salt
½ teaspoon ground black pepper
2 tablespoons half-and-half

CROUTONS

2 cups cubed bread, such as sourdough
1 tablespoon extra virgin olive oil
1 garlic clove, grated
½ teaspoon ground black pepper
¼ teaspoon fine sea salt

Preheat the oven to 425°F.

For the bisque, melt the butter in a large, heavy pot, such as a soup pot or Dutch oven. Add the onion and cook over medium-high heat until it begins to soften, about 3 minutes. Stir in the garlic.

Sprinkle in the flour and whisk until a paste forms. Continue to whisk as you slowly pour in the stock. Next, pour in the tomato sauce and add the sugar. Bring to a simmer and cook, partially covered, for 5 minutes.

Stir in the beer, salt, and pepper. Simmer for 5 more minutes. Remove from the heat. Stir in the half-and-half. Divide the soup between four bowls and sprinkle each with croutons before serving. This soup is best the same day it's made, but it can be stored in the refrigerator for up to 2 days.

To make the croutons, spread the bread cubes into a single layer on a baking sheet. Stir together the olive oil, garlic, pepper, and salt in a small dish. Drizzle it over the bread cubes and toss to coat.

Spread the cubes again into a single layer and bake for 7 minutes, stirring halfway through, until the croutons are browned and crisp.

Maibock Dutch Baby Pancake

with Berries

At first glance it looks impossibly elegant and impressive, but the Dutch Baby Pancake has everyone fooled. Not only is this brunch pastry delicious, it is simple to make. This version uses maibock, a spring beer, which offers toffee and caramel notes, and pairs well with the buttery pancake and the sweet spring berries.

SERVES 4 TO 6

PANCAKE
3 large eggs
½ cup unbleached all-purpose flour
2 tablespoons granulated sugar
¼ cup whole milk
2 ounces maibock
¼ teaspoon fine sea salt
3 tablespoons unsalted butter

TOPPING
1 tablespoon granulated sugar
¼ teaspoon ground cinnamon
½ cup diced strawberries
½ cup raspberries

Place a 10-inch skillet, preferably cast-iron, in the oven. Preheat the oven to 425°F.

Add the eggs, flour, sugar, and milk to a blender. Purée on high until smooth, about 10 to 15 seconds. Pour in the beer and add the salt. Purée until blended, about 10 more seconds.

Once the oven is preheated, carefully remove the hot skillet. Add the butter to the skillet and turn the pan to coat the bottom as it melts completely. Pour in the pancake batter.

Bake for 18 minutes, until puffed and golden brown. Remove from the oven and let sit for 5 minutes. In a small bowl, stir together the tablespoon of sugar and the cinnamon. Sprinkle it over the pancake and top with the berries. Slice and serve warm.

Maibock is a German spring beer sometimes called a Helles Bock. Beers to consider: Rogue Ales Dead Guy Ale, Yazoo Brewing Company Spring Seasonal Helles Bock, Summit Brewing Company Maibock

Quick Märzen Pecan Caramel Rolls

The last thing I want to do on a weekend morning is wait for a yeast bread to rise. This impatience has led to my love of quick rolls and biscuits, a breakfast treat that offers nearly instant gratification. I think they are best when coated in a nutty caramel sauce that is flavored with märzen, a traditional Oktoberfest beer. These rolls have a light texture but offer plenty of chewy caramel edges to enjoy.

MAKES 10 TO 12 SMALL ROLLS

ROLLS
2 cups unbleached all-purpose flour
1 teaspoon baking powder
½ teaspoon fine sea salt
⅓ cup cold unsalted butter, cubed, plus 1 tablespoon, softened
4 ounces märzen, room temperature
1 tablespoon packed dark brown sugar
½ teaspoon ground cinnamon

TOPPING
¼ cup packed dark brown sugar
2 tablespoons light corn syrup
2 tablespoons unsalted butter
1 ounce märzen
½ cup chopped raw pecans

 Märzen or Oktoberfest is a seasonal German beer available during autumn. Beers to consider: Brooklyn Brewery Brooklyn Oktoberfest, Great Lakes Brewing Company Oktoberfest, Sierra Nevada Brewing Company Oktoberfest

Preheat the oven to 375°F. Grease an 8-inch square pan with butter.

For the rolls, stir together the flour, baking powder, and salt in a medium bowl. Add the cubed butter. Use a pastry blender or two knives to work the butter into the flour until the mixture is in pea-sized pieces. Pour in 4 ounces of beer and stir until a dough forms. Knead the dough into a ball.

Roll the dough on a floured surface into a 9-by-12-inch rectangle. Turn the rectangle so that the long end faces you. Rub the softened tablespoon of butter over the dough. Sprinkle it with 1 tablespoon of the brown sugar and cinnamon. Start from the bottom and roll the dough into a log. Tuck in each end. Set aside.

For the topping, melt ¼ cup of the brown sugar, corn syrup, and 2 tablespoons butter in a small saucepan over medium-high heat, just until the sugar is dissolved, about 3 minutes. Remove from the heat. Stir in 1 ounce of beer. Return to medium heat and cook, stirring often until the sauce begins to thicken and coats the back of a spoon, 3 to 4 minutes. Adjust the temperature to keep the sauce from coming to a full boil, which will make the beer taste bitter.

Pour the sauce into the prepared baking pan. Sprinkle in the pecans.

Use a serrated knife to cut the log into 10 to 12 rolls. Place the rolls, cut side down, in the baking pan. Bake for 23 to 25 minutes, until the caramel sauce bubbles and the rolls are browned around the edges.

Remove from the oven and let the rolls cool for 5 minutes. Place a large platter or baking pan over the rolls. Invert the pan to release the rolls onto the platter. Scrape any extra caramel sauce out of the baking pan and onto the rolls. Serve warm.

Note: The berries need to soak for one hour, so be sure to plan ahead for this one.

Sour-Soaked Strawberry Muffins

The tart bite of a sour ale is balanced by the sweetness of strawberries in these muffins. The beer also gives the batter a light airiness that bakes into a tender breakfast treat. A fruity sour with strawberry or blackberry works well.

MAKES 12 MUFFINS

MUFFINS

1 pint strawberries, cored and diced
8 ounces sour beer
2 cups unbleached all-purpose flour, divided
2 teaspoons baking powder
½ teaspoon fine sea salt
4 tablespoons (½ stick) unsalted butter, melted
½ cup granulated sugar
1 large egg
⅓ cup chopped raw pecans

TOPPING

⅓ cup unbleached all-purpose flour
¼ cup packed dark brown sugar
¼ teaspoon cinnamon
¼ teaspoon fine sea salt
2 tablespoons cold unsalted butter, cubed

Beers to consider: Odell Brewing Company Friek, Firestone Walker Brewing Company Barrelworks SLOambic, New Belgium Brewing Company La Folie

Place the diced strawberries in a medium bowl and pour the beer over the berries. Cover and let sit at room temperature for one hour.

Preheat the oven to 400°F. Spray a standard 12-well muffin tin with nonstick cooking spray.

For the muffins, reserve 2 tablespoons of the 2 cups flour. Stir together the remaining flour, baking powder, and salt in a medium bowl. Set aside.

Stir together the melted butter and granulated sugar in a large bowl until smooth. Fold in the egg.

Strain the berries and reserve the beer. Stir the beer into the wet ingredients.

Gradually add the dry ingredients to the wet ingredients. Stir just until combined.

Sprinkle the reserved flour over the strawberries and add the pecans. Toss to coat the berries and nuts in the flour. Gently stir them into the muffin batter. Divide the batter between each of the 12 muffin wells in the prepared tin.

For the topping, stir all of the topping ingredients in a small bowl. Use a fork to break up the butter until evenly distributed throughout the flour and sugar, and the topping resembles a crumble. Add an equal amount to the top of each muffin.

Bake for 20 minutes, until a toothpick inserted into the center of the muffins comes out clean. Remove from the oven and set the muffin tin on a cooling rack to cool for 10 minutes. Remove them from the pan and enjoy. These muffins are best served the day they are baked, but they can be stored in an airtight container for up to 2 days.

Peanut Butter Stout Chocolate Chip Scones

STOUT

A stout lightens up the texture of these scones while adding a pleasant, slightly bitter chocolate flavor. A chocolate or a peanut butter stout adds a nice touch. A coffee stout will work, too. I tend to use white whole-wheat flour in my scones to add dense nuttiness. In this case, the flour goes especially well with the malty notes of the beer.

MAKES 8 SCONES

SCONES

2 cups white whole-wheat flour

2 teaspoons baking soda

2 tablespoons granulated sugar

½ teaspoon fine sea salt

½ cup (1 stick) cold unsalted butter, cubed, plus more for greasing

1 tablespoon unsweetened creamy peanut butter

6 ounces chocolate stout, room temperature

½ cup dark or semisweet chocolate chips

GLAZE

¾ cup confectioners' sugar, sifted

2 tablespoons unsweetened creamy peanut butter

1 ounce chocolate stout

Beers to consider: Belching Beaver Brewery Peanut Butter Milk Stout, High Water Brewing Campfire Stout, Modern Times Beer Black House Stout

Preheat the oven to 400°F. Grease a baking sheet with butter or cover it with a silicone baking mat.

Stir together the flour, baking soda, sugar, and salt in a large bowl. Add the butter and use a pastry blender or two knives to work the dough until the butter is in pea-sized pieces and evenly distributed throughout the flour.

Stir in the peanut butter. Add the beer and continue to stir. If necessary, use your hands to gently knead the dough together. Add the chocolate chips and work them into the dough. Form the dough into a disk about 7 inches in diameter. Place it on the prepared baking sheet and press any chocolate chips that may have escaped into the top of the dough.

Use a pastry cutter or knife to cut the disk into 8 equal wedges, but leave them in place on the baking sheet. Bake for 20 minutes, until the center of the scones are firm and the edges are slightly browned. Remove from the oven. Run a knife through the cut marks while the scones are still warm. Separate and transfer to a cooling rack to cool completely.

To make the glaze, stir together the confectioners' sugar and peanut butter in a small bowl. Add the beer 1 teaspoon at a time and continue to stir. You want a thick, but pourable glaze. Add more or less beer to reach this consistency.

Pour an equal amount of glaze over each scone. Use a spoon to gently spread some of the glaze, if necessary. Let the glaze set up, about 15 minutes, before serving. Store in an airtight container up to 2 days.

Chapter 4

TO GET STARTED

Game day dips and party appetizers are a natural fit for beer. I have all the favorites here, such as wings and salsa. But some of these standards use beers that will broaden your cooking horizons, such as porter in a smoked salmon spread and chile beer in salsa. Also, don't feel like you always need to keep things casual when it comes to cooking with beer. This section includes plenty of unexpected treats capable of impressing friends at your next cocktail mixer or dinner party.

Porter Smoked Salmon Spread

PORTER

Smoked fish dips are a party snack that need a much more prominent place at the table. They are one of my favorite things to spread over a cracker. Be sure to use a hot-smoked salmon for this recipe. Its firm texture, versus the delicate cold-smoked lox, blends well into a smooth spread with a malty flavor from the splash of porter. Smoked porter is ideal, but robust and brown porters are nice as well. Steer clear of dessert-inspired porters with descriptions like mocha or vanilla. This can be served with crackers, or it makes a nice filling for finger sandwiches.

SERVES 4 TO 6

1 tablespoon extra virgin olive oil
1 small onion, chopped (about ½ cup)
2 garlic cloves, minced
2 ounces porter
10 ounces hot-smoked salmon
8 ounces cream cheese, softened
Chopped fresh herbs such as dill or parsley, for garnish

Heat the olive oil in a medium skillet over medium-high heat. Add the onion and cook until it softens and begins to brown, about 5 minutes. Add the garlic and cook 1 more minute.

Reduce the heat to medium-low. Carefully pour in the beer. Continue to cook until very little liquid is left in the pan, 1 to 2 minutes. Remove from the heat.

Break the salmon into pieces and place in the bowl of a food processor. Add the cooked onions and any liquid left in the pan. Cover and pulse 3 to 4 times until the ingredients are finely chopped.

Add the cream cheese. Purée on high until ingredients combine into a smooth spread, about 20 seconds. Transfer to a serving bowl and sprinkle with chopped herbs. Store any extra spread in the refrigerator for up to 2 days.

Beers to consider: Alaskan Brewing Company Smoked Porter, Deschutes Brewery Black Butte Porter, Founders Brewing Company Porter

Three Cheese IPA Soup Shooters

The IPA is gently simmered in this soup, which helps to keep bitterness down while bringing out fresh herb and floral notes. These flavors blend well with sharp Cheddar and earthy goat cheese. An IPA with earthy or piney floral notes is a good pick. For less of a distinct beer bite, try a session IPA. This recipe will serve 4 to 6 as a starter, or soup shooters can serve many guests as a fun touch at a party.

MAKES 16 SHOOTERS

2 tablespoons unsalted butter
2 garlic cloves, grated
12 ounces IPA
1 tablespoon cornstarch
1 tablespoon water
8 ounces sharp Cheddar, shredded
2 ounces Monterey Jack, shredded
2 ounces soft goat cheese, crumbled
½ teaspoon Worcestershire sauce
¼ teaspoon ground black pepper
Finely chopped celery with leaves, for garnish

Melt the butter in a medium soup pot over medium-high heat. Add the garlic and cook until you begin to smell it, about 1 minute. Reduce the heat to medium and carefully add the beer.

Stir together the cornstarch and water in a small bowl. Whisk the slurry into the beer. Continue to whisk for 30 seconds to 1 minute. It will thicken slightly. Whisk in the Cheddar and Jack cheeses until melted. Whisk in the goat cheese until smooth.

Remove the soup from the heat and stir in the Worcestershire sauce and pepper.

Ladle the soup into shot glasses and garnish with chopped celery before serving.

Beers to consider: Bell's Brewery Two Hearted Ale, Bear Republic Brewing Company Racer 5 India Pale Ale, Stone Brewing Stone IPA

Chile Beer Tomatillo Salsa

I drink beer with my salsa, so why not beer in salsa? Chile beer to be exact, and it's my new go-to salsa ingredient. Any will do, but stick with light ales and lagers for this recipe versus a darker beer such as a chile-infused stout. Once the brew is added, the salsa is cooked only a couple of minutes so each bite hints at the spicy flavors of the beer. This salsa makes a great snack with chips, but you can also use it to top Mexican-inspired dishes like Baked Brown Ale Potato Cheddar Enchiladas (page 94).

SERVES 4 TO 6 AS A SNACK

1 pound tomatillos, quartered
1 small yellow onion, chopped (about ½ cup)
3 garlic cloves, chopped
2 yellow chile peppers (such as Santa Fe Grande), chopped
1 small red bell pepper, chopped
2 ounces chile beer
Juice of 1 lime
1 teaspoon granulated sugar
¾ teaspoon smoked sea salt
¼ cup chopped cilantro

Place the tomatillos, onion, garlic, yellow peppers, and bell pepper in a blender or food processor. Pulse in 5- to 10-second intervals until all ingredients are finely chopped. Transfer the salsa to a large nonstick saucepan.

Cook over medium-high heat for 5 minutes, stirring often. Pour in the beer, reduce the heat to medium, and cook for 2 more minutes. Stir in the lime juice, sugar, and smoked sea salt. Let the salsa cool completely. Stir in the cilantro just before serving. Store in an airtight container in the refrigerator for up to 3 days.

Note: The salsa can be eaten as soon as it is prepared and cooled, but it is even better when the flavors blend after 24 hours in the refrigerator.

Beers to consider: Tioga-Sequoia Brewing Company Joaquin Murrieta Chile Pepper Beer, Rogue Ales Chipotle Ale, Twisted Pine Brewing Company Billy's Chilies Beer

Pumpkin Ale Cheddar and White Bean Dip

★ ★ ★
PUMPKIN ALE

Don't be afraid of a strongly spiced pumpkin ale in this creamy dip. A holiday ale with similar spices to a pumpkin ale can also be used. Cinnamon and nutmeg blend surprisingly well with the cheeses and pumpkin. Serve it with tortilla chips or pretzels, but bagel chips and pita chips will work, too. Sip a lesser spiced amber ale or crisp pale ale while snacking.

SERVES 6 TO 8

One 15-ounce can low-sodium white beans, rinsed and drained
1 cup pumpkin purée
1 small yellow onion, chopped (about ½ cup)
3 garlic cloves, chopped
5 ounces sharp Cheddar, shredded, divided
2 ounces cream cheese, softened
2 ounces pumpkin ale
½ teaspoon fine sea salt
¼ teaspoon ground black pepper
Chopped fresh parsley and pumpkin seeds, for garnish

Preheat the oven to 375°F. Spray the baking dish with nonstick cooking spray.

Add the beans, pumpkin, onion, garlic, half of the Cheddar, and cream cheese to the bowl of a food processor. Pulse in 5- to 10-second intervals until all ingredients are blended.

Pour in the beer. Pulse again until the onions are finely chopped, but the beans are thick and a bit chunky. Stir in the salt and pepper.

Transfer the dip to the prepared baking dish. Place the baking dish on a baking sheet to catch any dip that may bubble over while baking. Sprinkle the remaining Cheddar over the top of the dip.

Bake for 28 to 30 minutes, until the dip is bubbling and the cheese begins to brown on the top. Let cool for 5 minutes before serving warm. Garnish with parsley and pumpkin seeds.

Note: You will need a 4-cup baking dish for this recipe. A crock or large ramekin works great, but an 8½-by-4½-inch loaf pan or even a 9-inch pie pan will suffice. I sometimes split the dip into two 2-cup ramekins. Just be aware that the baking time will decrease to about 25 minutes when you divide the dip between two baking dishes.

Beers to consider: Shipyard Brewing Company Pumpkinhead Ale, Buffalo Bill's Brewery Pumpkin Ale, Anderson Valley Brewing Company Fall Hornin'

Pilsner Quick Pickles

PILSNER

These beer pickles infuse the earthy flavors of dill and peppercorns with the crisp notes of a pilsner. Both German and Czech styles can be used. Serve them as part of a charcuterie platter and use them to top burgers, sausages, or Pilsner Pork Tenderloin Sandwiches (page 110).

MAKES 1 QUART JAR

1 English cucumber, cut into ¼-inch slices
½ small yellow onion, thinly sliced (about ¼ cup)
3 sprigs of dill
1 teaspoon black peppercorns
12 ounces pilsner
2 tablespoons granulated sugar
½ cup apple cider vinegar
½ teaspoon fine sea salt

Pack the cucumbers, onion, dill, and peppercorns into a clean quart mason jar.

Heat the beer and sugar to a simmer over medium-high heat in a medium saucepan. Simmer for 5 minutes. Stir in the vinegar and then the salt.

Pour the liquid into the jar and adjust the cucumbers to ensure all slices are submerged. Seal with a lid and refrigerate for at least 12 hours before enjoying. The pickles will stay fresh for up to 3 days.

Note: These pickles are quick to make, but they will need to rest in the refrigerator for at least 12 hours for the best flavor.

Beers to consider: Lagunitas Brewing Company Pils, Sierra Nevada Brewing Company Nooner Pilsner, Coney Island Brewing Company Mermaid Pilsner

Amber Ale French Onion Soup Dip

My husband's favorite soup is French onion, and the amber ale, New Belgium Brewing Fat Tire, ranks high on his craft beer list. It turns out that the nutty toasted notes and mild sweetness of the beer go nicely with the best part of this classic soup, the caramelized onions. To keep things interesting, I turned the two into a single appetizer. Serve this with slices of rye toast or pieces of freshly baked baguette for dipping. An amber ale is also a nice beer to enjoy with this snack.

SERVES 4 TO 6

4 tablespoons (½ stick) unsalted butter, divided
1 large yellow onion, diced (about 1 cup)
¼ teaspoon thyme leaves, minced
3 tablespoons unbleached all-purpose flour
½ cup beef stock
8 ounces amber ale
½ teaspoon fine sea salt
½ teaspoon ground black pepper
¼ cup panko bread crumbs
6 ounces Gruyère or Swiss cheese, shredded
Thyme sprig, for garnish

Melt 2 tablespoons of the butter over medium-high heat in a large skillet. Add the onion, reduce the heat to medium and cook, stirring occasionally, until the onions are soft and caramelized, about 45 minutes. Stir in the thyme.

Preheat the oven to 400°F and spray a 9-inch pie pan with nonstick cooking spray.

Return the skillet to medium-high heat and add the remaining 2 tablespoons of butter. Once it is melted and bubbling, sprinkle in the flour. Stir as the flour cooks and forms a paste around the onions, about 30 seconds. Slowly pour in the stock and continue to stir as it thickens.

Reduce the heat and carefully pour in the beer. Bring to a simmer, increasing the heat if necessary. Let simmer, stirring often, until thickened, about 2 more minutes. Stir in the salt and pepper, and then stir in the bread crumbs.

Pour the dip in the prepared pan. Top with cheese and bake for 20 minutes, until the cheese begins to melt and the dip is bubbling. Remove from the oven and let sit for 5 minutes before serving. Garnish with thyme sprig. Serve this dip warm soon after it comes out of the oven.

Beers to consider: New Belgium Brewing Company Fat Tire Amber Ale, Anderson Valley Brewing Company Boont Amber Ale, Rogue Ales American Amber Ale

Mexican Lager Shrimp Cocktail

Over the past couple of years, U.S. breweries have been putting their unique spin on the classic Mexican lager. Darker varieties, which are best here, have hints of malty, caramelized flavor and an amber color. It's a beer that blends well in the rich tomato broth of the traditional Mexican shrimp cocktail, a chilled soup filled with bits of cucumber, avocado, shrimp, and a twist of lime.

SERVES 6

2 pounds of fresh tomatoes, juiced to make about 2 cups
1 tablespoon granulated sugar
1½ teaspoons fine sea salt
12 ounces dark Mexican lager
2 tablespoons tomato paste
Juice of 4 limes (about ⅓ cup)
2 tablespoons Mexican hot sauce
5 scallions, green and white portions sliced
1½ cups halved cherry or grape tomatoes
1 English cucumber, diced (about 1¼ cups)
½ cup chopped cilantro
1 pound (60/70 count) cooked shrimp, tails removed
1 avocado, chopped

Combine the tomato juice, sugar, and salt in a medium saucepan and bring to a simmer over medium-high heat. Simmer for 5 minutes. Skim off any foam from the top with a large spoon and discard.

Pour the juice into a large bowl and let cool for 10 minutes, until no longer steaming. Pour in the beer and whisk in the tomato paste. Stir in the lime juice and hot sauce.

Add the scallions, cherry tomatoes, cucumber, cilantro, and shrimp, and stir well. Add the avocado. Cover and chill well, at least 4 hours. To serve, ladle an equal amount of shrimp and vegetables into each serving glass and top with the tomato juices left in the bowl. Because of the delicate avocado and acidic lime juice, this dish is best served the day it's made, but it can be stored in the refrigerator for up to 24 hours.

Note: This recipe uses juice made from fresh tomatoes. In a pinch, canned tomato juice will do. Stick with plain tomato juice, though, instead of tomato juice cocktails. They may contain seasonings and sugar that will overpower the final dish. The shrimp size listed is for cooked shrimp. If you are shopping for raw shrimp in the shell to cook yourself, look for 40/50 count or medium size.

Beers to consider: Oskar Blues Brewery Beerito Mexican Lager, Dust Bowl Brewing Company Taco Truck Amber Lager, 21st Amendment Brewery El Sully Mexican-Style Lager

Blonde Ale Honey Mustard Wings

BLONDE ALE

I have nothing against classic spicy Buffalo-style wings, but this is one appetizer that begs for experimentation. I enjoy the sauce almost more than the wings, so I'm always on the search for something creative. Blonde ale adds that special touch here. Choose a honey blonde ale, if it's available. When combined with mustard and honey, it creates a bold sauce for the chicken.

SERVES 6

3 pounds party wings and drumettes
½ teaspoon fine sea salt
2 tablespoons extra virgin olive oil
4 tablespoons unbleached all-purpose flour
2 tablespoons Dijon mustard
2 tablespoons honey
1 tablespoon hot sauce (any variety)
8 ounces blonde ale
1 tablespoon water
2 teaspoons cornstarch
¼ teaspoon ground black pepper
Chopped celery leaves, for garnish

Preheat the oven to 425°F. Cover a large baking sheet with parchment paper. Place the chicken in a large bowl and sprinkle with salt to season it lightly. Pour in the olive oil and stir to coat the chicken. Sprinkle in the flour and toss again to coat each piece.

Place the chicken pieces in a single layer on the parchment paper. Bake for 25 minutes. Remove the pan from the oven and use tongs to carefully flip each piece of chicken. Bake 25 more minutes, until golden brown and no longer pink.

While the chicken bakes, whisk together the mustard, honey, and hot sauce in a medium saucepan. Turn the heat to medium-high. Carefully add the beer and continue to whisk. Allow the sauce to come to a simmer.

While it cooks, stir together the water and cornstarch in a small dish. Whisk the slurry into the sauce. Continue to simmer and whisk until the sauce thickens, 5 to 7 minutes. Stir in the pepper. Remove from the heat and let cool for 2 to 3 minutes. It will thicken a little more.

Once the baked wings have been removed from the oven, pour the sauce over the wings on the baking sheet. Use tongs to turn and coat the wings in the sauce. Transfer to a serving platter and garnish with chopped celery leaves before serving. The wings are best enjoyed soon after they are prepared.

Beers to consider: Firestone Walker Brewing Company 805 Blonde Ale, Ska Brewing Company True Blonde Ale, Carson's Brewery Harlot Honey Blonde Ale

Pale Ale Marinara Meatballs

The best thing about these meatballs is all the ways you can serve them! The tender meatballs with beer-infused marinara make an easy party appetizer, but they are also a favorite for topping pasta and filling a sub roll for a hearty sandwich.

MAKES 24 MEATBALLS

MEATBALLS
2 garlic cloves, grated
1 tablespoon grated yellow onion
1 tablespoon finely chopped parsley
1 tablespoon finely chopped basil
1 pound lean ground beef
1 pound ground pork
1 ounce pale ale
¼ cup ground old-fashioned oats, or oat flour
1 teaspoon fine sea salt
¼ teaspoon ground black pepper

MARINARA SAUCE
2 tablespoons extra virgin olive oil
½ small yellow onion, finely diced (about ¼ cup)
2 garlic cloves, minced
2 tablespoons finely chopped basil
One 28-ounce can crushed tomatoes
11 ounces pale ale
1 tablespoon granulated sugar
1 teaspoon fine sea salt
¼ teaspoon ground black pepper
2 tablespoons freshly grated Parmesan, for garnish
Chopped basil, for garnish

Preheat the oven to 400°F.

To make the meatballs, stir together all meatball ingredients in a large bowl. Form the meat into 24 balls and place them on a large baking sheet covered in parchment paper or a silicone baking mat. Bake for 20 minutes, until browned and no longer pink in the middle.

While the meatballs bake, make the sauce. Heat the olive oil in a large heavy pot, such as a Dutch oven, over medium-high heat. Add the onion, garlic, and basil and cook until you begin to smell the garlic, about 1 minute. Reduce the heat to medium and stir in the tomatoes, and then the beer. Add the sugar, salt, and pepper. Simmer until the sauce begins to thicken, about 15 minutes.

Add the meatballs to the sauce and simmer over medium-low heat for 15 more minutes. Serve the meatballs warm with the sauce poured over them and garnish with the Parmesan and chopped basil. The meatballs and sauce can be stored in the refrigerator for up to 3 days.

Note: To save time, you can make the meatballs 24 hours ahead of time and bake just before serving. Store them on a baking sheet covered with plastic wrap in the refrigerator. Remove them from the fridge about 15 minutes before baking. To make ground oats simply pulse the rolled oats in a food processor until fine.

Beers to consider: Sierra Nevada Brewing Company
Pale Ale, Oskar Blues Brewery Dale's Pale Ale,
Deschutes Brewery Mirror Pond Pale Ale

Radish Toasts

with English Pale Ale Brown Butter

At the first sign of spring, I start craving sliced radishes on toasted sourdough with a spread of lightly salted butter. This appetizer only gets better when you put in the time to make brown butter. In this version, the butter is blended with a little English pale ale. This style of pale ale tends to hint at buttery notes, making it a pleasant fit for the nutty brown butter. An American pale ale can be used, but it will lack the buttery flavor. Enjoy drinking the leftover beer with your radish toast.

SERVES 4 TO 8

4 tablespoons (½ stick) unsalted butter
1 ounce English pale ale, room temperature
¼ teaspoon fine sea salt
8 slices sourdough bread, toasted
8 medium radishes, cut into 6 slices each
Chopped fennel fronds, for garnish
Flaked or coarse sea salt, for garnish

Place the butter in a small saucepan and melt over medium heat. Continue to cook the butter, swirling it in the pan, until it foams and darkens in color from gold to light brown, 2 to 3 minutes. Remove it from the heat once you begin to smell a nutty aroma.

Pour the butter into a heat-safe bowl. Pour only the butter and let most of the dark sediment remain in the saucepan to discard. Let the butter cool for 2 to 3 minutes and then whisk in the beer and salt.

Brush each slice of bread with the pale ale brown butter. Top each toast with 6 slices of radish. Drizzle on any remaining brown butter. Finish with a sprinkle of fennel fronds and sea salt before serving.

Beers to consider: Firestone Walker Brewing Company DBA (Double Barrel Ale), Big Sky Brewing Company Scape Goat Pale Ale, The Saint Louis Brewery Schlafly Pale Ale

Helles Herb Parmesan Pretzels

Beer will forever be associated with warm soft pretzels thanks to its German roots. No complaints here. A pretzel is my top pick among the bread and baked goods family. This pretzel recipe uses a traditional helles, which helps it to rise beautifully. Herbs and Parmesan add a savory touch.

MAKES 8 PRETZELS

PRETZELS

½ cup water, heated to 110 to 115°F

1 tablespoon granulated sugar

1 tablespoon dry active yeast

4¼ cups unbleached all-purpose flour

8 ounces helles, room temperature

4 tablespoons (½ stick) unsalted butter, melted

1 teaspoon chopped parsley

1 teaspoon chopped dill

1 teaspoon chopped chives

½ teaspoon fine sea salt

Extra virgin olive oil, for coating the bowl

WATER FOR BOILING

3 quarts water

⅔ cup baking soda

Stir together the warm water and the sugar, and then stir in the yeast. Let sit until the yeast blooms, 3 to 5 minutes.

Add the flour to the bowl of an electric mixer fitted with a dough hook attachment. With the mixer on low, pour in the yeast and then the beer. Continue to mix until combined, about 1 minute. Scrape the sides of the bowl as needed.

Mix in the melted butter and then add the parsley, dill, chives, and salt. Let the mixer knead the dough as it becomes a smooth ball in the center of the bowl, about 3 minutes. Transfer the dough to a floured surface and knead by hand until smooth and elastic, 3 to 5 more minutes. Roll into a ball. Coat a large bowl with extra virgin olive oil. Place the dough in the bowl. Cover with a clean dish towel and let rise in a draft-free place until doubled in size, about 1 hour.

Bring the 3 quarts of water and the baking soda to a boil in a large soup pot.

Punch down the dough and roll back into a ball. Cut into 8 equal pieces. Roll each piece into a thin cord, 22 to 24 inches long.

To make each pretzel, form the cord into a U shape. Bring both ends to touch and twist them together once or twice. Fold the ends back down to the base of the U shape and press them into the bottom of the pretzel.

Preheat the oven to 425°F. Cover two large baking sheets with parchment paper or a silicone baking mat.

continued

EGG WASH

1 large egg

1 tablespoon water

½ cup shredded Parmesan

Working one to two at a time, drop the pretzels in the boiling water. Boil until they float, 60 to 90 seconds. Remove with a slotted spoon and place on the baking sheet, about 4 pretzels on each sheet to allow for spreading while they bake.

Stir together the egg and 1 tablespoon of water in a small bowl. Brush each pretzel with the egg wash and sprinkle with Parmesan.

Bake for 12 minutes, until golden brown and baked through the center. Serve warm or at room temperature. Homemade pretzels are best eaten the same day, but they will stay fresh in an airtight container up to 24 hours.

Beers to consider: Victory Brewing Company Victory Helles Lager, Maui Brewing Co. Bikini Blonde Lager, Hangar 24 Craft Brewery Wheels Up Helles Lager. German Helles is sometimes called Munich Helles.

Roasted Winter Squash Soup

with Stout Brown Sugar Bacon

This creamy, rich soup makes a warming starter during the winter months. It's beer-heavy, but the bitterness of the stout is balanced by the sugar-coated bacon. Dry, Irish-style stouts or even a coffee stout is best. Avoid sweet or milk stouts. This soup is best the day it's made so plan to eat it right away.

SERVES 6 AS STARTERS

BACON

10 slices bacon (preferably low sugar and uncured)
6 ounces stout
1 cup packed light brown sugar

SOUP

2 tablespoons extra virgin olive oil
½ small yellow onion, finely chopped (about ¼ cup)
2 garlic cloves, minced
½ teaspoon ancho chile powder
¼ teaspoon ground black pepper
¼ teaspoon dried Mexican oregano
2⅓ cups puréed winter squash (about 2 acorn squash)
6 ounces stout
1½ cups low-sodium chicken or vegetable stock
1 teaspoon fine sea salt, or to taste

Note: I use roasted acorn squash, but any winter squash could be substituted. Canned squash purée is an acceptable substitute, but this soup is much more delicious with freshly roasted squash. To roast a squash, simply cut in half lengthwise. Remove the seeds, prick the skin with a fork, rub with olive oil, and roast on a baking sheet cut side down for 30 to 45 minutes at 400°F, or until tender. Cool, scoop out the flesh, and purée until smooth.

To make the bacon, preheat the oven to 350°F. Place a cooling rack over a baking sheet (place parchment paper on the baking sheet for easier clean up). Line the bacon in a shallow baking dish and pour in the beer. Let sit for 10 minutes.

Spread the brown sugar on a plate. Working one slice at a time, transfer the bacon to the brown sugar and coat well. Place the slice on the rack over the baking sheet. Repeat for all the slices. Bake for 25 to 30 minutes, or until it reaches your desired crispness. Remove from the oven. Let cool and then chop very fine.

To make the soup, heat the olive oil in a medium soup pot over medium-high heat. Add the onion and cook until it softens, about 3 minutes. Add the garlic and cook until it darkens slightly, about 2 minutes. Reduce the heat to medium-low.

continued

Sprinkle in the chile powder, pepper, and oregano. Stir to coat the onion and garlic. Stir in the squash. Slowly whisk in the beer and then the stock. Bring to a simmer and cook for 5 minutes.

Reserve one-quarter of the chopped bacon for garnish. Add the rest of the bacon to the soup. Taste and add the 1 teaspoon of salt, or more or less to taste.

Transfer to 6 serving cups and garnish with the reserved bacon.

Beers to consider: Mendocino Brewing Company Black Hawk Stout, Avery Brewing Company Out of Bounds Stout, Deschutes Brewery Obsidian Stout

Chapter 5

MEALS AND MAINS

T he main course is a craft beer's best friend; the place where it can truly shine. Stews, pizza crusts, and batters can allow for a greater volume of your favorite brew. You can add an extra hit of the good stuff to your sauces to enhance the best qualities of the beer, from mild hoppy bitterness to sweet caramelization. You'll find both meaty main courses and vegetarian options in this section, because beer is an ingredient that does its best to please everyone.

American Wheat and White Bean Stew

Wheat beer gives this filling vegetarian stew a hint of citrus that pairs well with the earthy rosemary used to flavor the broth during slow cooking. Serve it as a warming meal with a hunk of rustic bread, or top it with a poached egg. Just remember to plan ahead with this one because the white beans will need to soak overnight.

MAKES 4 TO 6 SERVINGS

1 pound dried white beans, soaked in water overnight
2 large carrots, sliced
1 large yellow onion, diced
22 ounces American wheat ale
2 cups water
Two 3- to 4-inch sprigs of rosemary
1 teaspoon fine sea salt
½ teaspoon ground black pepper

Drain and rinse the beans, and add them to the bowl of a slow cooker (about 6 quarts in size). Add the carrots and onion. Pour in the beer and water. Stir to combine all ingredients. Place the rosemary sprigs in the liquid.

Cover the slow cooker with the lid and cook on low for 8 hours or until the beans reach your desired tenderness. Stir in the salt and pepper. Serve warm. Leftovers will keep up to 2 days in the fridge.

Note: If you need to speed up the soaking process, you can use the quick soak or hot soak method. Place the beans in a large pot and add 10 cups of water. Boil for 2 to 3 minutes. Drain and rinse the beans for use. You can also opt to remove beans from the heat and let them sit in the hot water for at least 4 hours. Soaking methods can influence cooking times. For example, leaving the beans in hot water for an extended period can reduce the long overall cooking time that is needed when using a slow cooker.

Beers to consider: Bell's Brewery Oberon Ale, Lagunitas Brewing Company A Little Sumpin' Sumpin' Ale, Tioga-Sequoia Brewing Company Half Dome California Wheat. A hefeweizen will work, but it will add a bit more sweetness.

Autumn Oktoberfest Fish Stew

This stew is a meal that welcomes fall weather and seasonal Oktoberfest beers. Tender sweet potatoes are cooked with chopped fish in a beer broth with a malty character and is balanced by a touch of sweetness from coconut milk. Choose a firm white fish like cod or halibut because it will stay in more uniform cubes while cooking. Honey Blonde Dinner Rolls with Blonde Honey Butter (page 126) make a great addition to this stew.

SERVES 4

1 tablespoon extra virgin olive oil
1 tablespoon unsalted butter
1 large yellow onion, chopped
4 garlic cloves, minced
1 pound sweet potatoes, peeled and cubed (about 3 cups)
2 cups water
8 ounces Oktoberfest beer
8 to 10 ounces firm white fish, cubed
⅓ cup coconut milk
¾ teaspoon fine sea salt
¼ teaspoon ground black pepper
½ teaspoon finely chopped rosemary

Heat the olive oil and butter over medium-high heat in a large, heavy pot, such as a Dutch oven. Once the butter is melted, add the onion and cook until browned and softened, about 7 minutes. Add the garlic and cook 1 more minute. Stir in the sweet potatoes and cook until the color brightens, about 2 minutes.

Pour in the water and bring the stew to a simmer. Partially cover the pot with a lid and cook until the potatoes are barely fork-tender, about 5 minutes. Reduce the heat to medium and stir in the beer.

Carefully drop in the chopped fish and cook just until it turns opaque. Remove the stew from the heat. Pour in the coconut milk and stir in the salt, pepper, and rosemary. Serve warm. Leftovers will keep up to 2 days in the fridge.

Beers to consider: Brooklyn Brewery Brooklyn Oktoberfest, Great Lakes Brewing Company Oktoberfest, Sierra Nevada Brewing Company Oktoberfest

Barleywine Beef Short Rib Stew

with Herbed Rice

Boneless short ribs are my top pick for making beef stew. When cooked low and slow they always end up perfectly tender without the tough, stringy quality often found in other cuts. Barleywine adds a sweetness to this stew that combines with the vegetables and herbed rice to create the ultimate comfort food. Look for a barleywine-style ale versus a high-alcohol barrel-aged barleywine. Beers labeled as English barleywines can be used.

SERVES 4 TO 6

RIBS

1 cup beef broth
6 ounces barleywine
¼ cup packed light brown sugar
½ teaspoon fine sea salt, plus extra
    for seasoning meat
¼ teaspoon ground black pepper,
    plus extra for seasoning meat
1 tablespoon extra virgin olive oil
4 large carrots, peeled and cut into
    1½-inch pieces (about 1 pound)
1 pound fingerling potatoes
1 large yellow onion, cut into 8
    wedges
Two 4-inch sprigs of thyme

Preheat the oven to 300°F.

Stir together the beef broth, barleywine, brown sugar, ½ teaspoon salt, and ¼ teaspoon pepper in a medium bowl. Set aside.

Heat the oil in a large, heavy-bottomed pot with a lid, such as a Dutch oven, over medium-high heat. Sprinkle one side of the ribs generously with salt and pepper. Place the ribs seasoned side down in the oil, cook until browned on one side, about 2 minutes. Season the top of the ribs with salt and pepper and then flip and cook until browned on the other side, about 2 minutes. Turn off the heat.

Use tongs to gently lift the ribs in case they are stuck to the bottom of the pot. Pour in the broth and beer liquid. Arrange the carrots, potatoes, and onion around and on top of the ribs. Place the thyme sprigs on top of the vegetables.

Cover the pot. Bake for 2 hours 30 minutes, until the ribs are fall-apart tender. Discard the thyme.

continued

RICE

1 tablespoon extra virgin olive oil
2 garlic cloves, minced
1 cup dry long grain white rice
3 cups water
1 tablespoon chopped parsley
1 teaspoon chopped dill
½ teaspoon fine sea salt

About 30 minutes before the stew is cooked, make the rice. Heat the 1 tablespoon of oil in a large pot over medium-high heat. Add the garlic and cook just until it begins to brown, about 2 minutes. Add the rice and stir to coat it in the oil.

Reduce the heat to medium and pour in the water. Bring the rice to a simmer. Partially cover with a lid and simmer until the liquid is absorbed and the rice is tender, about 15 minutes. Cover with the lid and let sit for 5 minutes. Fluff the rice with a fork. Stir in the parsley, dill, and salt.

Divide the rice into 4 to 6 servings. Top with an equal amount of the beef stew with vegetables. Serve warm. Leftovers will keep in the fridge for up to 3 days.

Beers to consider: Anchor Brewing Company Old Foghorn Ale, Sierra Nevada Brewing Company Bigfoot Barleywine Style Ale, AleSmith Brewing Company Old Numbskull Barleywine Ale

Slow-Cooked 5-Spice Stout Shredded Chicken

STOUT

The roasted chocolate notes of a stout emerge when it is slow cooked with meats to create deeply flavored sauce. A spiced stout, chocolate stout, or coffee stout are a nice fit for this recipe, but avoid milk or sweet stouts. The spices used here bring to mind Asian five spice powders, creating a fusion of flavors ideal for banh mi–style sandwiches. I've included what you'll need to create those sandwiches in this variation. Opt for a lighter, more refreshing beer when you enjoy this chicken, such as a pale ale or hefeweizen.

SERVES 4 TO 6

SAUCE
2 dried guajillo chilies (see note, page 93)
½ cup tomato sauce
4 garlic cloves, chopped
12 ounces stout
½ teaspoon fine sea salt
¼ teaspoon ground black pepper

SPICE PACK
1 cinnamon stick
3 whole star anise
1 teaspoon coriander pods
½ teaspoon whole cloves
½ teaspoon black peppercorns

CHICKEN
¼ cup unbleached all-purpose flour
½ teaspoon fine sea salt
¼ teaspoon ground black pepper
2 pounds boneless chicken thigh
    fillets

To make the sauce, toast the chilies in a dry skillet over medium-high heat, tossing them gently in the pan until you begin to smell them, about 3 minutes. Transfer them to a deep, heatproof bowl. Bring 2 cups of water to a boil. Pour the water over the chilies and let sit submerged for 30 minutes.

Place the tomato sauce and garlic in a small blender or food processor. Once the chilies are softened, drain the water. Discard the stem and seeds, and roughly chop. Add the chilies to the blender.

Pulse for 10- to 15-second intervals until everything is finely chopped. Add the stout, ½ teaspoon of salt, and ¼ teaspoon of black pepper. Purée until smooth, about 20 seconds.

To make the spice pack, place all spices in the center of a 6-inch square of cheesecloth. Wrap the cloth around the spices to make a pouch and tie off the end.

To make the chicken, stir together the flour, ½ teaspoon of salt, and ¼ teaspoon of black pepper in a shallow bowl. Dredge the chicken in the flour to coat each piece. Arrange the chicken in the bottom of a slow cooker (about 6 quarts in size).

continued

Pour the sauce over the chicken. Add the spice pack. Cover with a lid and cook on high for 4 hours or until the chicken is fork-tender. Remove the spice pack. Shred the chicken using two forks and let it soak in the sauce until ready to serve. Leftovers can be stored in the fridge for up to 3 days.

Note: Feel free to substitute another dried chile pepper, such as aji panca or puya, if the guajillo chile is not to your liking. Just be sure to do some research on the variety you choose as heat levels can vary greatly.

Variation: The chicken recipe will make four banh mi-style sandwiches. You will need 4 rolls or buns and 4 tablespoons of mayonnaise. For toppings, I like to use sliced cucumbers, cilantro, and pickled vegetables such as carrots and daikon. You can add diced or sliced hot chile peppers for heat. To assemble, spread the bun with 1 tablespoon of mayonnaise, add the chicken, and pile on your favorite vegetables.

Beers to consider: Sierra Nevada Brewing Company Stout, BarrelHouse Brewing Company Stout, Deschutes Brewery Obsidian Stout

Baked Brown Ale Potato Cheddar Enchiladas

AMERICAN BROWN ALE

Homemade Mexican food meets a comforting casserole with these enchiladas. Brown ale deepens the flavors and brings out the best in the rich tomato-based enchilada sauce. This beer is also a good beverage to serve alongside the meal. The recipe calls for baked potatoes. To save time, I typically microwave them until tender.

SERVES 6

POTATOES

1 tablespoon unsalted butter

1 small yellow onion, chopped

2 garlic cloves, minced

2 medium russet potatoes (about 1 pound), baked

2 large gold potatoes (about 1 pound), baked

½ teaspoon fine sea salt

¼ teaspoon smoked paprika

3 ounces brown ale

8 ounces white or yellow Cheddar, shredded, divided

Preheat the oven to 400°F. Spray a 9-by-13-inch baking dish with nonstick cooking spray.

To make the enchilada filling, melt 1 tablespoon of butter in a large skillet over medium-high heat. Add the onion and cook until it begins to soften, about 3 minutes. Add the garlic and cook for 1 more minute.

Roughly chop the baked potatoes (with the skin on, unless you choose to discard it) and add them to the skillet. Stir in the salt and the smoked paprika. Pour in the 3 ounces of beer and stir the potatoes, gently breaking them up. Cook until the liquid is absorbed and any remaining evaporates, about 1 more minute. Sprinkle with half of the cheese. Let cool.

continued

SAUCE

2 tablespoons unsalted butter

1 tablespoon unbleached all-purpose flour

3 tablespoons chile powder

3 tablespoons tomato paste

9 ounces brown ale

1 cup low-sodium chicken stock

½ cup tomato sauce

1 teaspoon ground cumin

1 teaspoon dried oregano

½ teaspoon garlic powder

½ teaspoon fine sea salt

¼ teaspoon smoked paprika

12 large corn tortillas, warmed

Chopped cilantro, for garnish

To make the sauce, melt the 2 tablespoons of butter in a medium saucepan over medium-high heat. Once melted, sprinkle in the flour and whisk it into a paste, about 30 seconds. Whisk in the chile powder and then the tomato paste. A thick red paste should form.

Carefully pour in the 9 ounces of beer and then the stock as you continue to whisk. Bring to a low simmer and cook until it begins to thicken slightly, 5 minutes. Add the tomato sauce, and then stir in the cumin, oregano, garlic powder, salt, and paprika. Continue to simmer for 5 more minutes.

Transfer ¼ cup of the sauce to the baking dish and spread it to coat the bottom. Work on a flat surface and scoop an equal amount of potato filling into the bottom center portion of a tortilla. Roll from the bottom up and place seam side down in the baking dish. Continue with the remaining tortillas. It's okay if the tortillas split in some spots once you get it into the baking dish.

Pour the remaining sauce over the enchiladas and sprinkle with the remaining cheese. Bake for 12 minutes, until the cheese is melted and the enchiladas are bubbling. Serve warm, sprinkled with cilantro. Leftovers will keep in the fridge for up to 2 days.

Note: Look for corn tortillas that are 7 to 8 inches in diameter. I often find them labeled as large corn tortillas. If you can't find them, feel free to substitute with flour. You can also use smaller corn tortillas and make more enchiladas with less potato filling inside each one.

Beers to consider: Big Sky Brewing Company Moose Drool Brown Ale, Avery Brewing Company Ellie's Brown Ale, Figueroa Mountain Brewing Company Davy Brown Ale. Beers labeled as English brown ales can also be used.

Nachos

with Roasted Chilies and IPA Beer Cheese Sauce

INDIA PALE ALE

The hoppy bite of IPA makes an outstanding cheese sauce. It takes some care to ensure the hoppy goodness doesn't turn bitter, but cooking it slowly brings out the best in this style of brew. A hoppy, fruity IPA is best. For less of a beer punch, try a session IPA. I also sometimes make this cheese sauce using a Mexican-style lager. These nachos are kept simple with roasted chilies to allow the cheese sauce to shine, but feel free to add more of your favorite nacho toppings. I also like to eat my nachos with a hoppy glass of IPA.

SERVES 4 TO 6

NACHOS
1 large yellow onion, cut into 8 wedges
2 Anaheim chilies
2 yellow chilies (such as Santa Fe Grande)
1 poblano pepper
2 tablespoons extra virgin olive oil
Pinch of fine sea salt
Pinch of ground black pepper
One 14-ounce bag tortilla chips
2 medium tomatoes, cored and diced
2 cups shredded green cabbage
¼ cup chopped cilantro
4 to 6 lime wedges, for garnish

CHEESE SAUCE
3 tablespoons unsalted butter
3 tablespoons all-purpose flour
½ cup whole milk
5 ounces IPA
10 ounces sharp Cheddar, shredded
¼ teaspoon fine sea salt
Pinch ground black pepper

Preheat the oven to 425°F.

For the roasted vegetables, arrange the onion wedges and chilies on a baking sheet. Drizzle with olive oil and toss to coat. Bake for 10 minutes and then use tongs to carefully stir the onions and flip the chilies. Bake for 10 more minutes, until the chilies are softened, blackened in some spots, and the skins begin to separate. Sprinkle on the pinch of salt and black pepper. Transfer the chilies to a zip-top bag and seal.

Let the chilies cool about 15 minutes, until they are cool enough to handle. Remove them from the bag. Remove any loose skins and discard. Chop the chilies and discard the stems and seeds. Chop the onion.

Make the beer cheese sauce. Melt the butter in a medium saucepan over medium-high heat. Reduce the heat to medium and sprinkle in the flour. Whisk vigorously until a paste forms and let cook for about 60 seconds. Continue to whisk as you pour in the milk. Whisk until smooth.

Remove the pan from the heat and whisk in the beer. Begin to stir in the cheese a handful at a time, allowing each addition to melt before adding the next. Once the cheese stops melting, return the pan to medium-low heat. Continue to stir in the cheese until it has all been added and melted. The result should be a creamy, pourable cheese sauce. Stir in the ¼ teaspoon of salt and pinch of black pepper.

continued

Arrange the tortilla chips on a serving tray. Drizzle the sauce over the chips then sprinkle with the chopped onions and peppers. Next, layer on the tomatoes, cabbage, and cilantro. Garnish with lime wedges and serve.

Note: You will want the peppers and cheese sauce to be warm when served. Make the peppers first and keep them on the stove in a skillet set over low heat while you make the cheese sauce. Then assemble the nachos as soon as the cheese sauce is done. It's also worth noting that homemade cheese sauce doesn't always have the same consistency as sauce from a store-bought can. It's okay if your IPA sauce has a tiny bit of texture visible while cooking. You won't think a thing of it once you sneak a taste.

Beers to consider: Founders Brewing Company All Day IPA, Stone Brewing Stone IPA, West Sixth Brewing IPA

California Common Fig and Walnut Flatbread

After living in California for 5 years now, figs, walnuts, and California common, or steam beer, immediately come to mind when I think of the state. This recipe combines these ingredients in a chewy flatbread crust. It makes a great meal when served with a salad, or cut it into small squares to serve as a party appetizer.

SERVES 4 TO 6 AS A MAIN COURSE

CRUST

1 cup cake flour
1 cup unbleached all-purpose flour
1 teaspoon granulated sugar
½ teaspoon fine sea salt
6 ounces California common beer, room temperature
Extra virgin olive oil for coating bowl and pizza pan
1 tablespoon yellow cornmeal

SPREAD

8 dried black mission figs, quartered
6 ounces California common beer
2 tablespoons extra virgin olive oil, divided
1 shallot, thinly sliced
2 garlic cloves, chopped
½ teaspoon fine sea salt

To make the crust, add the flours to the bowl of an electric mixer fitted with a dough hook attachment. Sprinkle in the sugar and salt. Turn the mixer to low and pour in the beer. Allow the mixer to knead the dough on medium speed for 2 minutes. It should form a ball in the center of the bowl.

Turn the dough out onto a floured surface and knead until smooth, about 2 more minutes. Coat a medium-size bowl with olive oil. Form the dough into a ball and place the dough in the bowl. Cover with a clean dish towel and place in a draft-free spot for 1 hour. It will rise only slightly, by 30 to 50 percent.

While the dough rises, place the figs in a small saucepan. Add the beer and bring to a simmer over medium heat. Remove from the heat and let sit for 15 minutes.

Heat 1 tablespoon of the olive oil over medium-high heat in a small skillet. Add the shallot and cook until softened, about 5 minutes. Add the garlic and cook 3 more minutes. Sprinkle with ½ teaspoon of the salt.

Transfer the figs and liquid to a small food processor or single-serving blender. Add the shallots and garlic along with the remaining 1 tablespoon of olive oil. Purée into a spreadable paste.

Preheat the oven to 425°F. Coat a 16-inch round pizza pan with olive oil and sprinkle with the cornmeal. Spread the dough to a 13- to 14-inch

TOPPINGS

1½ cups thinly sliced radicchio
½ cup crumbled blue cheese
¼ cup chopped walnuts, toasted

circle on the pizza pan. Spread the fig purée over the dough. Bake for 20 minutes, until the edges are crisp and slightly browned.

Top the flatbread with radicchio, blue cheese, and walnuts. Cut into squares and serve warm or at room temperature.

Beers to consider: Anchor Brewing Company Anchor Steam Beer, Anchor Brewing Company Anchor Dry-Hopped Steam Beer, Smuttynose Brewing Company East Coast Common

Maibock Mushroom, Caramelized Onion, and Goat Cheese Sliders

The maibock is light and slightly hoppy. It offers a nice variation to the darker porters and stouts that are often used in rich mushroom dishes. The beer lightens up the flavor of these sliders, which allows them to pair well with earthy goat cheese. These sliders are an ideal remedy for a chilly spring day that still requires comfort food. Serve a glass of maibock with your sliders or try a refreshing pilsner.

MAKES 8 SLIDERS

2 tablespoons unsalted butter
1 large yellow onion, sliced
8 ounces sliced white button
    mushrooms
4 ounces maibock
¼ teaspoon fine sea salt
¼ teaspoon ground black pepper
4 ounces soft goat cheese
¼ teaspoon cracked black pepper
¼ teaspoon thyme leaves, minced
8 slider buns or rolls

Melt the butter over medium-high heat in a large skillet. Add the onion. Reduce the heat to medium and cook for 30 minutes, stirring occasionally. The onions will soften and begin to turn golden brown. If they begin to darken too quickly, reduce the heat. They should be browned and soft, but not mushy.

Add the mushrooms and continue to cook until the onions are very soft and the mushrooms are dark and tender, about 10 minutes. Stir in the beer and cook 2 more minutes to heat it through. Sprinkle with salt and ground pepper.

Use a fork to mix together the goat cheese, cracked black pepper, and thyme in a small bowl, until the cheese is crumbly and the seasonings are evenly distributed.

Sprinkle or spread the bottom portion of each slider bun with goat cheese. Top with the caramelized onions and mushrooms. Cover with the top portion of the bun and serve. The mushrooms and onions can be stored in the fridge for up to 3 days.

Maibock is a German spring beer, sometimes called a Helles Bock. Beers to consider: Rogue Ales Dead Guy Ale, Yazoo Brewing Company Spring Seasonal Helles Bock, Summit Brewing Company Maibock

Cheesy Shrimp and Bacon Pale Ale Pasta

with Green Peas

You can't go wrong with pasta, cheese, and beer. They are ingredients that always play well together. The light pale ale cheese sauce in this recipe delicately coats the pasta for a meal that's hearty, but not too heavy. Feel free to serve this meal with a pint of pale ale.

SERVES 4 TO 6

16 ounces pasta

4 slices thick-cut bacon, diced

1 pound 40/50 count medium raw shrimp, cleaned and tails removed

½ small yellow onion, finely chopped

2 tablespoons unbleached all-purpose flour

4 ounces pale ale

2 ounces sharp Cheddar, shredded

¼ teaspoon fine sea salt

¼ teaspoon ground black pepper

½ cup fresh or thawed green peas

Fill a large pot with water for your pasta. Turn to high and heat to boiling while you begin the pasta sauce.

For the pasta sauce, cook the bacon over medium-high heat in a large, heavy-bottomed pot, such as a Dutch oven, until the fat renders and the bacon begins to brown, about 4 minutes. Continue to cook for 2 to 3 more minutes, until it reaches your desired crispness. Add the shrimp and cook until opaque, about 2 more minutes. Remove the pot from the heat and use a slotted spoon to transfer the bacon and shrimp to a bowl, leaving the bacon grease behind.

Add the pasta to the boiling water and cook according to package directions while you finish the sauce.

Return the pot with bacon grease to medium-high heat and add the onion. Cook until it begins to soften, about 2 minutes. Sprinkle in the flour and whisk it into a dry paste. Reduce the heat to low. Continue to whisk as you pour in the pale ale. It will thicken into a paste as it simmers, about 30 seconds. Stir in the cheese, salt, and pepper until the cheese melts. Increase the heat to medium-low if the cheese slows its melting.

Drain the pasta, but reserve the pasta water. Add the hot pasta to the sauce with ½ cup of the pasta water. Toss to coat the pasta with the sauce. If the sauce seems thick, add ¼ to ½ cup more pasta water.

Stir in the peas. Transfer an equal amount of pasta to each serving bowl. Top with shrimp and bacon and toss gently in the bowls before serving. Leftovers will keep for up to 2 days in the refrigerator.

Beers to consider: Sierra Nevada Brewing Company Pale Ale, Oskar Blues Brewery Dale's Pale Ale, Deschutes Brewery Mirror Pond Pale Ale. A less hoppy British pale ale works in this recipe, too.

Note: I like to use spaghetti in this recipe, but you can substitute any variety of your favorite pasta.

Cast-Iron Pilsner Pizza

with Beer Marinara, Smoked Mozzarella, and Arugula

PILSNER

While I don't mind a thin-crust pizza every now and then, I remain a true fan of a thick crust that is balanced with tender chewiness and a crisp bottom. The combination of beer as a leavening agent and a cast-iron skillet make the perfect version of this pizza every time. This pizza is topped with a beer marinara, and the sweet graininess and slightly flora hoppiness of a pilsner adds a contrast to the acidic tomatoes. You can use any of your favorite toppings, but I prefer smoky mozzarella and peppery arugula. A crisp pilsner or a blonde ale also serves as a great pairing for this pizza.

SERVES 4 TO 6

CRUST

2 teaspoons granulated sugar
¼ cup water, heated to 110 to 115°F
2 teaspoons dry active yeast
2½ cups unbleached, all-purpose flour
½ cup yellow cornmeal
7 ounces pilsner, room temperature
¼ teaspoon fine sea salt
2 tablespoons extra virgin olive oil, plus extra for coating the bowl
8 ounces smoked mozzarella, sliced or shredded
1 cup arugula

SAUCE

1 cup tomato sauce
5 ounces pilsner
1 clove garlic, grated
2 teaspoons granulated sugar
½ teaspoon fine sea salt
¼ teaspoon ground black pepper
8 basil leaves, minced

Stir the sugar into the warmed water. Stir in the yeast and let bloom, about 5 minutes.

Add the flour to the bowl of an electric mixer fitted with a dough hook. Stir in the cornmeal. With the mixer on low, add the bloomed yeast. Pour in the beer and increase the mixer speed to medium. Add the salt and allow the dough to knead in the mixer for 3 minutes. It should form a ball in the center of the bowl.

Turn the dough out onto a floured surface and knead until smooth and elastic, about 2 more minutes. Coat a large bowl with olive oil. Place the dough in the bowl, cover with a clean dish towel, and let rise in a draft-free spot until doubled in size, about 1 hour.

While the dough rises, make the sauce. Stir together all the sauce ingredients in a medium saucepan. Bring it to a simmer over medium-high heat. Simmer for 10 minutes to blend the flavors and slightly thicken it. Set it aside to cool.

Preheat the oven to 450°F. Place a 10-inch cast-iron skillet over medium-high heat on the stove. Add 2 tablespoons of olive oil to coat the pan. Once warmed, remove from the heat.

Punch the dough down. Place it in the warmed cast-iron skillet and spread it evenly along the bottom. Top with the marinara sauce and the mozzarella. Bake for 20 to 25 minutes, until the edges are browned and crust is baked through.

Top with arugula and serve warm. The pizza is best eaten right out of the oven, but it will keep in the fridge for up to 2 days.

Both German and Czech styles make tasty pizza.
Beers to consider: Sierra Nevada Brewing Company Nooner Pils, North Coast Brewing Company Scrimshaw Pilsner Style Beer, Coney Island Brewing Company Mermaid Pilsner

Lambic Barbecue Ground Bison Subs

The fruity, sweet flavors of a lambic mimic that of a sweet and smoky barbecue sauce. In this recipe, the beer is used to make a homemade sauce that surrounds the meaty ground bison. Choose one that is fruity and sweet, and slightly tart. If you can't find a U.S. version, check out the Belgian imports section in your market. This is a quick and simple sandwich that makes for an easy weeknight dinner. Enjoy these sandwiches with a smoky Scottish ale or try a malty amber ale.

SERVES 3 TO 4

1 pound ground bison
1 large yellow onion, finely chopped
1 garlic clove, minced
4 ounces lambic
3 tablespoons tomato paste
1 tablespoon light or dark molasses
½ teaspoon fine sea salt
¼ teaspoon smoked paprika
¼ teaspoon ground black pepper
3 to 4 sub buns
Chopped red onion and jalapeños, for garnish

Cook the bison in a large, deep skillet over medium-high heat until it begins to brown, about 2 minutes. Add the onion and garlic. Continue to cook until the bison is browned and no longer pink, 6 to 8 more minutes.

Reduce the heat to low. Pour in the beer and then stir in the tomato paste and molasses. Stir well to coat all of the ground meat. Add the salt, paprika, and black pepper. Increase the heat to medium and cook until all ingredients are heated through, about 1 more minute.

Fill each bun with an equal amount of ground bison. Sprinkle with red onion and jalapeños before serving. The ground meat will keep up to 3 days in the refrigerator.

Beers to consider: Brouwerij Lindemans Framboise, Upland Brewing Company Cherry Lambic, High Water Brewing Ramble on Rose

Pilsner Pork Tenderloin Sandwiches

PILSNER

I grew up in Indiana, one of a handful of Midwestern states that claim to be home of the pork tenderloin sandwich. You will rarely find a fair or long-standing restaurant without this sandwich on the menu with its thin and crispy fried meat and standard store-bought hamburger bun. This version is my beer-friendly ode to the original. The tenderloin is pounded thin and then marinated for 30 minutes in pilsner and seasonings before being breaded and fried. This sandwich pairs well with just about any light beer from the pilsner to a hoppy IPA. Be sure to top each sandwich with a few Pilsner Quick Pickles (page 64) before serving.

SERVES 4

4 thinly cut boneless pork chops
    (about 1 pound)
12 ounces pilsner
2 garlic cloves, grated
1 teaspoon ground mustard
¼ teaspoon fine ground sea salt,
    plus more for seasoning the
    cooked pork chops
¼ cup unbleached all-purpose flour
1 large egg, beaten
1 cup panko bread crumbs
Peanut oil for frying (or oil of your
    preference)
4 hamburger or sandwich buns

Place a pork chop between 2 sheets of plastic wrap and use a meat tenderizer to pound it to ¼ inch thickness. Repeat for the remaining pork chops and place them in a casserole dish.

Whisk together the pilsner, garlic, mustard, and the ¼ teaspoon of salt in a bowl. Pour the marinade over the pork chops and turn them to coat evenly. Cover and place in the refrigerator to rest for 30 minutes.

Place the flour, egg, and bread crumbs each in their own shallow bowl. Fill a heavy-bottomed pot with ½ to 1 inch of cooking oil and heat over medium-high heat until it sizzles when you drop in some bread crumbs.

Drain the pork chops and discard the marinade. Dredge each chop in the flour and then the egg. Turn to coat it evenly with bread crumbs. Fry until golden brown and cooked through, about 3 minutes on each side. Transfer the pork to a sheet pan covered in paper towels to absorb the excess oil. Sprinkle with salt. Repeat with the remaining pork slices.

Serve warm on a bun.

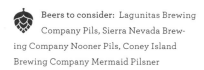 **Beers to consider:** Lagunitas Brewing Company Pils, Sierra Nevada Brewing Company Nooner Pils, Coney Island Brewing Company Mermaid Pilsner

Lentil Burgers
with Wheat Beer Barbecue Sauce

I like my vegetarian burgers with a good sauce for serving. This wheat beer barbecue sauce adds the perfect touch to these lentil and nut burgers. I prefer to use a German-style hefeweizen. I usually eat them on their own or with a salad, but piling one up with toppings on a sourdough bun is also a great way to go.

SERVES 6

BURGERS

3 cups water
1 cup brown lentils
1 tablespoon olive oil
1 small yellow onion, chopped
2 ounces wheat ale
½ cup chopped walnuts
½ teaspoon fine sea salt, or to taste
¼ teaspoon ground black pepper, or to taste

BARBECUE SAUCE

10 ounces wheat ale
½ cup tomato sauce
2 garlic cloves, grated
2 tablespoons light brown sugar
1 tablespoon Dijon mustard
1 tablespoon light or dark molasses
½ teaspoon fine sea salt
¼ teaspoon ground black pepper

Beers to consider: Sierra Nevada Brewing Company Kellerweis, Widmer Brothers Brewing Hefeweizen, Golden Road Brewing Hefeweizen

Combine the water and lentils in a medium saucepan. Bring to a boil over medium-high heat. Reduce the heat to a simmer, and partially cover the pan with a lid. Cook until the lentils are tender, about 20 minutes. Drain if any water remains. Set aside to cool.

Heat the olive oil in a medium skillet over medium-high heat. Add the onion and cook until softened and it begins to brown, about 5 minutes. Reduce the heat to medium and carefully add the beer. Stir to deglaze the pan and cook until most of the liquid evaporates, about 3 minutes.

Preheat the oven to 400°F.

Transfer the cooled lentils to a food processor. Add the onions and any liquid that remains in the pan. Add the walnuts, salt, and pepper. Pulse in 10-second intervals 3 or 4 times, until all ingredients are chopped and hold together when formed into a ball. You can taste the mix at this point and add more salt and pepper, if desired.

Form the mix into 6 equal-sized patties. Place on a baking sheet covered with parchment paper or a silicone baking mat. Bake for 20 minutes, until the edges are golden brown. Let the burgers rest on the pan for 5 minutes before moving.

While the burgers bake, whisk together all the sauce ingredients in a medium saucepan. Heat over medium-high heat to a simmer. Reduce the heat to medium-low and simmer for 30 to 35 minutes, stirring occasionally. Watch it closely the last 5 minutes as it will begin to thicken into a barbecue sauce and will need to be stirred more often to avoid burning. Reduce the heat as needed.

Serve the burgers warm with the sauce on the side. Both the burgers and sauce will keep in the refrigerator for up to 3 days.

Chapter 6

ON THE SIDE

A good side dish can make the meal. It's why I believe that life should not be wasted on bland steamed vegetables and rice pilafs. This doesn't mean you shouldn't eat your greens, but it does mean you should add a little beer. From salads to beans and potatoes, these side dishes stand up to their important supporting role.

Red Ale Roasted Potatoes

RED ALE OR AMBER ALE

Roasted red potatoes are my favorite go-to side dish. The key to getting the edges nice and crispy is a hot oven and giving them plenty of time to roast. This slightly spicy version gets a touch of malty flavor from a splash of red ale. The best option is an ale prominent with toasted malt notes.

SERVES 4 TO 6

1 pound red potatoes, cut into 1-inch cubes (about 4 large potatoes)
1 teaspoon ground cumin
1 teaspoon dried oregano
1 teaspoon fine sea salt
½ teaspoon smoked paprika
½ teaspoon ground turmeric
¼ teaspoon ground cayenne pepper
1 ounce red ale
1 teaspoon extra virgin olive oil

Preheat the oven to 425°F.

Place the potatoes in a large bowl. Stir together the cumin, oregano, salt, paprika, turmeric, and cayenne in a small dish. Mix in the beer and olive oil.

Pour over the potatoes and toss well to coat. Spray a baking sheet with nonstick cooking spray. Spread the potatoes in a single layer on the baking sheet. Bake for 20 minutes. Carefully remove the pan from the oven and stir. Bake for 15 to 20 more minutes, until the potatoes are tender and their edges are browned and crisp.

Beers to consider: 21st Amendment Brewery Toaster Pastry, Kona Brewing Company Lavaman Red Ale, Mendocino Brewing Company Red Tail Ale

Crispy Brussels Sprouts and Spinach Salad

with Orange IPA Roasted Garlic Dressing

I first had crispy Brussels sprouts leaves mixed into a salad at one of my favorite brewpubs. The texture of the crunchy leaves with tender spinach was so memorable, and I knew right away that I wanted to re-create something similar. An IPA salad dressing highlights the citrus and brings it all together. Choose an IPA with citrus notes. A session IPA is also an option.

SERVES 4 TO 6

DRESSING
1 head garlic
⅓ cup extra virgin olive oil
3 ounces IPA
3 tablespoons fresh orange juice
2 tablespoons chopped walnuts
1 tablespoon granulated sugar
¼ teaspoon fine sea salt
¼ teaspoon ground black pepper

SALAD
1½ pounds Brussels sprouts
2 tablespoons extra virgin olive oil, divided
¼ teaspoon fine sea salt
¼ teaspoon ground black pepper
3 cups fresh spinach
Segments from 1 navel orange, chopped

Beers to consider: Deschutes Brewery Fresh Squeezed IPA, Dogfish Head Craft Brewery 60 Minute IPA, Founders Brewing Company All Day IPA

Cut the top third off the head of garlic. Place the head, cut side up, on a piece of foil large enough to wrap the garlic. Drizzle with 1 tablespoon of the olive oil and wrap the head of garlic in the foil. Place it in the oven. Turn the oven to 425°F and set the timer to 30 minutes.

For the salad, prep the Brussels sprouts by trimming the bottom one-third off each one and then work from the bottom to remove the leaves. Remove as many as you can and then cut the tender center core in half and add it to the leaves.

Lay the Brussels sprouts leaves in a single layer on a baking sheet. Drizzle with 1 tablespoon of olive oil and sprinkle with ¼ teaspoon each of salt and pepper.

Once the 30 minutes has passed, leave the garlic in the oven and place the Brussels sprouts in the oven. Bake for 10 minutes then stir the leaves. Bake for 10 more minutes, or until most of the leaves are dark and crisp. Remove from the oven and set aside. Remove the garlic when you remove the Brussels sprouts.

Add the spinach to a large bowl. Transfer the Brussels sprouts to the bowl and add the orange segments.

Once the garlic is cool enough to handle, squeeze the roasted cloves into a small food processor or single-serving blender. Add the remaining dressing ingredients and purée until smooth. Just before serving, pour half the dressing over the salad and toss to combine. Serve the remaining dressing on the side.

Note: This salad can easily be turned into a full meal and will serve about two. Consider adding chickpeas, shrimp, or grilled chicken to make it a little more filling.

Wheat Berry Salad
with Miso-Witbier Dressing

A witbier with notes of bright citrus works well in salad dressings. Here, a little lemon juice and lemon zest really pull the citrus in the beer while the miso adds salty balance with a hint of creaminess. Beer dressings work especially well with cold grain salads. I keep things simple here with only wheat berries and scallions, but for a heartier side dish, or even a meal, stir in halved cherry tomatoes, diced marinated tofu, or leftover shredded chicken.

SERVES 4 TO 6

2½ cups cooked wheat berries
    (about 1 cup dry)
4 scallions, green and white
    portions sliced
2 tablespoons white miso
1 ounce witbier
1 teaspoon honey
¼ teaspoon lemon zest
½ teaspoon fresh lemon juice
¼ teaspoon ground black pepper

Toss the cooked wheat berries and the scallions in a medium bowl.

In a small bowl, whisk together the miso and beer until smooth. Whisk in the honey and then add the lemon zest and lemon juice. Sprinkle in the pepper. Continue to whisk until the dressing is smooth, about 30 seconds.

Pour the dressing over the wheat berries and stir to combine all ingredients. Serve at room temperature or cold. The salad will keep in an airtight container in the refrigerator for up to 2 days.

Note: White miso is sometimes called Hawaiian-style miso. It is mellower in flavor than yellow or red miso.

Beers to consider: Allagash Brewing Company Allagash White, Lagunitas Brewing Company Stoopid Wit, Boston Beer Company Samuel Adams White Ale

Grilled Romaine Salad

with Pale Ale Parmesan Dressing

This salad is easy to add to any grilling menu. Prepare the dressing before you start cooking and then toss the lettuce on the grill once your meat and other vegetables are done. The pale ale combined with lemon creates a burst of citrus in the creamy, herb dressing. Choose a hoppy pale ale with strong citrus notes. If you don't have a grill, you can re-create this salad using a large grill pan on the stove. It just won't have the same smoky flavor.

SERVES 4

¼ cup freshly grated Parmesan
1 garlic clove, chopped
4 tablespoons sour cream
2 tablespoons mayonnaise
1 tablespoon chopped parsley
1 teaspoon lemon zest
¼ teaspoon fine sea salt
Pinch ground black pepper
2 ounces pale ale
Cooking oil for the grill
1 large head romaine lettuce
Shaved Parmesan and lemon
    wedges, for garnish

Place the grated Parmesan, garlic, sour cream, mayonnaise, parsley, lemon zest, salt, and pepper in a small food processor or single-serving blender cup. Purée until all ingredients are combined, about 15 seconds. Pour in the beer, purée until smooth, another 10 to 15 seconds.

Heat the grill to medium-high to high, about 400°F. Brush the grate with oil. Place the head of lettuce on the grill. Use tongs to flip it every 15 seconds, until the outer leaves begin to darken and wilt. It will take about 5 minutes.

Place the lettuce on a cutting board and chop into large pieces. Transfer to a serving bowl, pour in the dressing, and toss to coat. Garnish with shaved Parmesan and lemon wedges before serving.

Note: The goal with a grilled romaine salad is to cook the lettuce just until the outer leaves are warmed and slightly wilted while the inner head stays cool and crisp. When it's chopped together, it creates a mix of temperatures and textures.

Beers to consider: Sierra Nevada Brewing Company Pale Ale, Stone Brewing Pale Ale 2.0, Deschutes Brewery Mirror Pond Pale Ale

Chile Beer Cast-Iron Corn Bread

I like my corn bread on the spicy side, which makes chile beer an excellent addition. The heat of the beer tends to lessen when it's mixed into the corn bread so don't be afraid to go bold and choose a spicy brew. A lager-style chile beer is a good choice, but a chile-infused stout, even a chile saison, are also options. The result is a dense, cakey corn bread loaded with rich buttery flavor and a hint of robust beer.

SERVES 8 TO 10

1½ cups medium-ground yellow cornmeal

1 cup unbleached all-purpose flour

2 tablespoons granulated sugar

2 teaspoons baking powder

½ teaspoon fine sea salt

½ cup chopped pickled jalapeños

2 garlic cloves, minced

2 scallions, green and white portion sliced, divided

4 tablespoons (½ stick) unsalted butter, melted, plus 2 tablespoons, softened

1 large egg, beaten

12 ounces chile beer

Preheat the oven to 375°F. Place an 8-inch cast-iron skillet in the oven.

Stir together the cornmeal, flour, sugar, baking powder, and salt. Toss in the chopped jalapeños and garlic. Reserve a tablespoon of scallions for garnish, and then add the rest to the bowl. Toss to coat them in the dry ingredients. Stir in the ¼ cup melted butter and then the egg. Pour in the beer and stir just until all ingredients are combined.

Carefully remove the hot skillet from the oven. Drop 1 tablespoon of the softened butter into the skillet. Move it around with a spatula so that it melts and coats the bottom of the skillet evenly.

Pour the batter into the skillet. Bake for 28 to 30 minutes, until edges begin to brown and a toothpick inserted into the center comes out clean. Remove from the oven and spread the remaining 1 tablespoon of butter over the top of the warm corn bread. Garnish with the reserved scallions. Cut the corn bread into wedges. Serve warm or at room temperature. Keep in an airtight container for up to 2 days.

Beers to consider: Tioga-Sequoia Brewing Company Joaquin Murrieta Chile Pepper Beer, Rogue Ales Chipotle Ale, Twisted Pine Brewing Company Billy's Chilies

Honey Blonde Dinner Rolls

★★★
BLONDE
ALE

with Blonde Honey Butter

These dinner rolls are made tender with the addition of blonde ale, and they are drenched in a spiked honey butter as soon as they come out of the oven. Choose a honey blonde if you can find one. Serve them with Summer Saison Tomato Bisque with Garlic–Black Pepper Croutons (page 44) or the Autumn Oktoberfest Fish Stew (page 87).

SERVES 9

ROLLS

1 tablespoon honey
1 teaspoon active dry yeast
¼ cup water, heated to 110 to 115°F
2¼ cups unbleached all-purpose flour
4 ounces blonde ale, plus 1 teaspoon
½ teaspoon fine sea salt
Softened butter to coat bowl and baking pan

HONEY BUTTER

1½ tablespoons unsalted butter, softened
1 teaspoon honey
1 teaspoon blonde ale, room temperature
Pinch of fine sea salt

Stir the honey and yeast into warm water. Let it sit to bloom, about 5 minutes.

Add the flour to the bowl of an electric mixer fitted with a dough hook attachment. With the mixer on low, pour in the bloomed yeast. Pour in the 4 ounces of beer. Mix on medium until the dough comes together, about 1 minute. If the dough is a little dry and crumbly, add the additional 1 teaspoon of beer. Mix in the salt.

Let the mixer knead the dough on medium speed until smooth, 3 to 4 minutes. Transfer the dough to a floured surface and knead by hand until smooth and elastic, about 5 minutes. Form the dough into a ball. Coat the inside of a large bowl with softened butter. Place the dough ball in the bowl and cover with a clean dish towel. Let rest in a draft-free spot until doubled in size, about 1 hour.

Once it has doubled, punch down the dough and knead it back into a ball on a floured surface. Cut the dough into 9 equal pieces. Grease a 9-inch cake pan with butter. Roll each piece into a ball and place them in the prepared pan.

Preheat the oven to 400°F.

Place the pan on the stove while the oven heats up. Let rise for 20 minutes, they will puff up slightly. Bake until golden brown, about 12 minutes.

While the rolls bake, make the honey butter by whisking the butter, honey, and blonde ale together in a small dish. Add the pinch of salt.

Remove the rolls from the oven, brush with the honey butter. Enjoy warm.

Beers to consider: Firestone Walker Brewing Company 805 Blonde Ale, Ska Brewing Company True Blonde Ale, Carson's Brewery Harlot Honey Blonde Ale

Brown Ale Baked Beans

AMERICAN BROWN ALE

I love baked beans, but many versions are too sweet for my preference. These beans use a malty brown ale with honey, which creates a more complex and savory taste versus an overwhelming sugary-sweet flavor. Beers labeled as English brown ales can also be used.

SERVES 6 TO 8

1 tablespoon unsalted butter

1 small yellow onion, diced

1 cup dried black beans, soaked in water overnight

1 cup dried pinto beans, soaked in water overnight

1 cup dried small red beans, soaked in water overnight

4½ cups water

12 ounces brown ale

One 6-ounce can tomato paste

2 tablespoons honey

2 tablespoons Dijon mustard

2 teaspoons fine sea salt

1 teaspoon garlic powder

1 teaspoon ground black pepper

¼ teaspoon smoked paprika

Preheat the oven to 350°F.

Heat the butter in a large deep pot with a lid, such as a Dutch oven. Add the onion and cook until the onion begins to soften and brown, about 5 minutes. Remove from the heat.

Rinse and drain the soaked beans and add them to the pot. Then stir in the water, beer, tomato paste, honey, and mustard. Mix in the salt, garlic powder, pepper, and paprika.

Cover with the lid and bake for 2 hours 15 minutes to 2 hours 30 minutes, until the beans become tender. Remove the lid and bake for 10 more minutes to allow the sauce to thicken. Serve warm. Leftovers will keep in the refrigerator for up to 3 days.

Note: Plan ahead with this one as the beans need to be soaked overnight. For quick soak methods see American Wheat and White Bean Stew (page 84). Feel free to use any variety of your favorite dried beans, but cooking times may vary.

Beers to consider: Big Sky Brewing Company Moose Drool Brown Ale, Avery Brewing Company Ellie's Brown Ale, Figueroa Mountain Brewing Company Davy Brown Ale

Stout and Maple Glazed Sweet Potato Slices

In this recipe, thick slices of sweet potatoes are brushed as they bake with a glaze made of stout and maple syrup. The stout adds a deep nutty and somewhat chocolatey flavor to the tender potato slices. It makes a simple side dish for the fall and holiday season. Milk stouts aren't the best choice here, but a stout with vanilla, chocolate, or honey notes works well.

SERVES 4 TO 6

4 sweet potatoes (about 1 pound), cut into ¾-inch thick slices
2 tablespoons unsalted butter, melted
2 tablespoons pure maple syrup
1 ounce stout
¼ teaspoon fine ground sea salt
¼ cup chopped raw walnuts

Preheat the oven to 425°F.

Place the potato slices in a single layer on a large baking sheet covered with parchment paper or a silicone baking mat.

Stir together the butter, maple syrup, stout, and salt in a small dish. Brush the potatoes with the glaze and bake for 5 minutes. Carefully flip the potato slices and brush with the glaze again. Bake for 5 more minutes. Continue to bake, flip, and brush the potatoes every 5 minutes, until they are tender, about 20 minutes total.

While the potatoes bake, place the walnuts in a small skillet and toast over medium-high heat, tossing them gently in the skillet. Toast until you begin to smell the nutty aroma, 3 to 5 minutes.

Once the potatoes are done baking, brush with the remaining glaze. Transfer to a serving plate and top with the toasted walnuts. Serve warm.

Beers to consider: Sierra Nevada Brewing Company Stout, BarrelHouse Brewing Company Stout, Deschutes Brewery Obsidian Stout

Warm IPA Braised Cabbage Salad

with Pastrami and Swiss

INDIA PALE ALE

My all-time favorite sandwich is the Reuben and this salad came about as a lighter way to enjoy similar flavors. The splash of IPA gives a floral, hoppy punch to the warm cabbage that sweetens slightly as it's sautéed. A hoppy IPA with earthy or piney floral notes is a good pick. This is balanced by the saltiness of the pastrami and Swiss cheese. Corned beef can be swapped for the pastrami. I made the switch to pastrami because in some areas corned beef can be difficult to find outside of the month of March.

SERVES 6

1 tablespoon extra virgin olive oil
1 medium head green cabbage, thinly sliced (about 8 cups)
3 to 4 ounces IPA
¼ teaspoon fine sea salt
¼ teaspoon ground black pepper
¼ pound sliced pastrami, chopped
6 ounces Swiss cheese, cubed

Heat the olive oil in a large pot, such as a Dutch oven, over medium-high heat. Add the cabbage. Turn to coat it in the oil. Reduce the heat to medium. Carefully pour in 3 ounces of the beer. Cook, stirring often, until the cabbage begins to wilt and the liquid has evaporated, 4 to 6 minutes. If you would like the cabbage softer, add more beer and continue to cook to reach your desired texture. Stir in the salt and pepper.

Transfer the cabbage to a serving bowl. Toss in the pastrami and Swiss cheese. Serve warm.

Beers to consider: Bell's Brewery Two Hearted Ale, Bear Republic Brewing Company Racer 5 India Pale Ale, Stone Brewing Stone IPA

Pilsner Battered Fried Summer Squash Slices

with Creamy Ranch Beer Dip

Fried zucchini was a regular on our summer menus when I was growing up. My mom would slice the zucchini that my dad brought in from the garden, coat it in flour, and skillet-fry it until it was soft in the middle and crunchy on the outside. I've added my own twist to that family favorite by dipping thick slices in a beer batter made with a light and crisp pilsner. The batter puffs up with crunchy edges and the zucchini stays a bit firm for a little extra bite. The slices are paired with a ranch-style dip spiked with a little more refreshing pilsner.

SERVES 8 TO 10

ZUCCHINI

3 medium zucchini, cut into half-inch slices (about 1½ pounds)
1½ cups unbleached all-purpose flour
10 ounces pilsner
½ teaspoon fine sea salt, plus more to season cooked zucchini
¼ teaspoon garlic powder
Peanut oil for frying (or your preference of oil)

DIP

⅔ cup sour cream
3 tablespoons mayonnaise
2 garlic cloves, chopped
2 tablespoons chopped dill
1 tablespoon chopped chives
¼ teaspoon fine sea salt
2 ounces pilsner

Place paper towels over a large baking sheet and arrange the zucchini cut side down on the paper towels. Place another paper towel on top and press gently to absorb some of the moisture. Let the zucchini sit on the paper towels while you make the dip.

Add the sour cream, mayonnaise, garlic, dill, chives, and salt to a small food processor or the cup of a single-serving blender. Pulse 3 to 4 times to chop all ingredients.

Pour in the beer. Purée until smooth, about 15 seconds. Pour the dip into a bowl, cover, and refrigerate until ready to serve.

For the zucchini, whisk together the flour and beer in a medium bowl until smooth. Add the salt and garlic powder.

Fill a deep heavy pot with 3 inches of oil and heat to 375°F. Alternatively, you can use an electric fryer. Fill and heat to the manufacturer's instructions.

Work in batches and dip the zucchini slices into the batter turning to coat them evenly. Drain off excess batter and then carefully drop the slices into the oil, about 4 at a time. Fry until golden brown, 3 to 4 minutes. Remove the zucchini from the oil with a slotted spoon and transfer to a clean sheet pan covered in paper towels to absorb excess oil. Sprinkle each slice with salt.

Serve warm with the sauce on the side.

Beers to consider: Sierra Nevada Brewing Company Nooner Pils, North Coast Brewing Company Scrimshaw Pilsner Style Beer, Coney Island Brewing Company Mermaid Pilsner

Wild Rice
with Dried Cranberries, Porter, and Pecans

PORTER ★★★

With nutty wild rice and cranberries, this recipe is worthy of the holiday table. The fruit and nuts are soaked in porter to give the whole dish notes of roasted, chocolate flavor. Choose a nutty brown porter or a robust chocolatey porter. I use wild rice because I love the chewy texture and nutty flavor, but any blend of rice or grains can be substituted. Just be sure to cook the grains you choose according to their package directions before adding them to the skillet with the other ingredients.

SERVES 4

3 cups water
1 cup wild rice
½ cup dried cranberries
½ cup pecan halves
4 ounces porter
1 tablespoon unsalted butter
1 small yellow onion, chopped

Boil the water in a medium pot over medium-high heat. Add the rice, reduce the heat to a strong simmer, and partially cover the pan with a lid. Cook the rice until tender, about 45 minutes. Drain any excess liquid.

While the rice cooks, place the cranberries and pecans in a medium bowl. Pour in the porter and let soak for 15 minutes.

Melt the butter in a large, deep skillet over medium-high heat. Add the onion. Cook until it begins to soften, about 3 minutes. Add the rice. Reduce the heat to medium and carefully add the cranberries and pecans with the soaking liquid.

Return the heat to medium-high and cook until the liquid has evaporated and all ingredients are heated through, about 2 minutes. Serve warm. Leftovers will keep in the fridge for up to 2 days.

Beers to consider: Deschutes Brewery Black Butte Porter, Founders Brewing Company Porter, Smuttynose Brewing Company Robust Porter

Carrot Ribbons

with Brown Ale and Bacon

AMERICAN BROWN ALE

I'll admit, I'm not the biggest fan of cooked carrots. But cut them into thin ribbons, add beer and bacon, and they become a side dish I look forward to. There is just a splash of brown ale in this recipe. It's enough to add nutty, toffee notes to the brown sugar that is well balanced by bites of smoked bacon. Beers labeled as English brown ales can also be used.

SERVES 4

3 large carrots
3 slices thick-cut bacon, chopped
1 teaspoon light brown sugar
1 ounce brown ale
Pinch of fine sea salt
Pinch of ground black pepper

Peel the carrots, and then use the peeler to shave the carrots into long ribbons. You should end up with about 3 cups of carrot ribbons.

Add the bacon to a medium skillet heated over medium-high heat. Cook until the bacon begins to bubble and the fat renders. Continue to cook until the bacon pieces reach your desired crispness, 5 to 7 minutes. Watch the bacon carefully during the last couple of minutes of cooking as it can brown and burn quickly. Adjust the heat as needed.

Reduce the heat to medium-low, stir in the brown sugar and then the beer. Add the carrot ribbons and cook just until they begin to soften, about 1 minute. Stir in the salt and pepper. Serve warm.

Beers to consider: Big Sky Brewing Company Moose Drool Brown Ale, Avery Brewing Company Ellie's Brown Ale, Figueroa Mountain Brewing Company Davy Brown Ale

Chapter 7

I'LL HAVE DESSERT

M aybe it's the fun names on the labels or my mad sweet tooth, but I am naturally drawn to beer styles that work well in desserts. Don't think for a second, though, that the beers themselves have to be sweet. It's true that coconut porters and gingerbread stouts are begging for a baked treat, but Scottish ales, saisons, and IPAs also have their place among the final course.

Bourbon Barrel–Aged Blondies

The sweet, oaky notes of a bourbon barrel–aged beer go well with just about any dessert, and blondies are an especially good fit. Look for an aged brown ale, stout, or porter. I turn to blondies often because they are quick, require few ingredients, and always get rave reviews.

SERVES 9

½ cup (1 stick) unsalted butter, melted
1 cup packed light brown sugar
1 large egg
¼ teaspoon fine sea salt
1 ounce bourbon barrel–aged beer
1 cup unbleached all-purpose flour
⅓ cup chopped raw pecans

Preheat the oven to 350°F. Grease an 8-inch square pan with butter.

Stir together the melted butter and brown sugar in a medium bowl until combined. Fold in the egg until blended. Add the salt, and then stir in the beer.

Gradually add the flour and stir just until all the ingredients are combined in a smooth batter. Pour the batter into the prepared pan. Sprinkle the pecans evenly over the blondies.

Bake for 20 minutes, until a toothpick inserted into the center comes out clean. Let cool for 10 minutes before cutting to serve. Store in an airtight container for up to 2 days.

Beers to consider: New Holland Brewing Dragon's Milk Bourbon Barrel Stout, Avery Brewing Company Vanilla Bean Stout, Anderson Valley Brewing Company Wild Turkey Bourbon Barrel Stout

Cream Ale Vanilla Bean Bundt Cake

with Cream Cheese Frosting

A stout might seem like the most familiar choice for a cake, but once you make a vanilla cake with cream ale, you will change your mind. This cake is full of vanilla and the beer keeps it light and tender. Any cream ale will work, but a cream ale infused with vanilla or other dessert flavor will be even better. Easy to transport and slice, this bundt cake makes a great choice for potlucks and parties.

SERVES 12 TO 14

CAKE

2½ cups cake flour
½ teaspoon baking soda
½ teaspoon fine sea salt
1½ cups granulated sugar
1 cup (2 sticks) unsalted butter, melted and cooled
3 large eggs
1 vanilla bean, divided, for use in both the cake and the frosting
4 ounces cream ale

Preheat the oven to 350°F. Grease a 10-inch fluted tube or Bundt pan with butter and dust with all-purpose flour or cake flour.

Stir together the flour, baking soda, and salt in a medium bowl.

Add the sugar and melted butter to the bowl of an electric mixer. Mix on medium until combined, about 1 minute. With the mixer on low, add the eggs one at a time. Increase the speed to medium and mix until the eggs are blended into the batter, about 30 more seconds.

Slit the vanilla bean. Scrape the inside to gather about one quarter of the vanilla bean paste and set aside for the frosting. Scrape the rest of the paste from the bean and add it to the mixer.

With the mixer on low, pour in the beer. Scrape the side of the bowl as needed and continue to mix until smooth, about 30 seconds.

Add the dry ingredients to the mixer a little at a time and mix just until everything is combined, about 30 more seconds.

Pour the batter into the prepared pan. Bake for 40 minutes, or until a toothpick inserted into the center comes out clean. Remove from the oven and let the pan cool on a cooling rack for 30 minutes. Use a knife to loosen the edges of the cake. Place a serving plate over the bottom of the cake pan and invert to release the cake from the pan. Let the cake cool completely, about 1 hour.

continued

FROSTING

1 cup confectioners' sugar
3 ounces cream cheese, softened
6 teaspoons whole milk

To make the frosting, add the confectioners' sugar, cream cheese, and reserved vanilla paste to the bowl of the mixer. Blend on medium and then medium-high until a thick paste forms, about 2 minutes.

Add the milk, 1 to 2 teaspoons at a time, increasing the speed to medium-high between each addition. Mix until the frosting begins to lighten and becomes thin enough to spread over the cake, about 1 more minute.

Once the cake is cool, pour the frosting over the top and use a spatula to gently spread it to drape over the sides. Serve right away. Store leftovers in the refrigerator for up to 2 days.

Beers to consider: Mother Earth Brew Company Cali Creamin' Vanilla Cream Ale, Buffalo Bill's Brewery Orange Blossom Cream Ale, Sixpoint Brewery C.R.E.A.M. Cream Ale Brewed with Coffee

Gingerbread Stout Bars

with Brown Butter Frosting

The nutty brown butter frosting in this recipe spreads like velvet over these decadent spiced cake bars. They are full of holiday flavors, but one bite and you might find yourself making them every season of the year! Look for a holiday or gingerbread stout around the holidays, but any dessert or coffee stout works well. Serve these with a taster of the rich dessert stout used in the recipe.

SERVES 9

BARS

1 cup whole-wheat flour
½ teaspoon baking powder
¼ teaspoon ground cinnamon
¼ teaspoon ground nutmeg
¼ teaspoon fine sea salt
¼ teaspoon ground black pepper
Pinch ground clove
1 cup (2 sticks) unsalted butter, softened
⅔ cup packed light brown sugar
1 large egg
1 tablespoon light or dark molasses
2 ounces stout
1½ teaspoons freshly grated ginger

Preheat the oven to 350°F. Line an 8-inch square baking pan with parchment paper so that one inch extends beyond the edge of the pan on all sides.

Stir together the flour, baking powder, cinnamon, nutmeg, salt, pepper, and clove in a medium bowl. Set aside.

Blend together the butter and brown sugar in an electric mixer on medium-high until light and creamy, about 3 minutes. Scrape the sides of the bowl as needed. Mix in the egg and then the molasses. Continue with the mixer on medium-low to medium as you add the beer. The batter may appear a bit lumpy (that's okay). Add the ginger.

Gradually add the dry ingredients a little at a time with the mixer on low. Increase the speed to medium and mix just until all ingredients are combined.

Pour the batter into the prepared baking pan and spread evenly. Bake for 28 to 30 minutes, until a toothpick inserted in the center comes out clean. Let the bars cool completely.

continued

FROSTING

2 tablespoons unsalted butter
2 cups confectioners' sugar
4 tablespoons whole milk
¼ teaspoon pure vanilla extract
Pinch of fine sea salt

While the bars cool, begin the frosting. Melt the butter in a small saucepan over medium heat. Swirl the butter in the pan as it foams and as dark specks begin to form and you smell a nutty aroma, 2 to 3 minutes. Remove from the heat and let cool.

Add the cooled butter (with the brown specks) to the bowl of an electric mixer. Add the confectioners' sugar, one cup at a time, and mix until dry and crumbly. With the mixer on low, add 1 to 2 tablespoons of milk. Turn the mixer to high and whip the frosting. Add the additional milk, a little at a time, to reach a spreadable consistency. Mix in the vanilla and salt.

Frost the cooled bars evenly and cut into 9 squares before serving. Bars can be stored in the refrigerator for up to 2 days.

Beers to consider: Golden Road Brewing Back Home Gingerbread Stout, Hardywood Park Craft Brewery Hardywood Gingerbread Stout, Stone Brewing Xocoveza Winter-Spiced Mocha Stout

Oatmeal Raisin and Barleywine Cookies

AMERICAN BARLEYWINE

Barleywines tend to have rich toffee notes that hint at raisin as they linger on your tongue. It makes me think of oatmeal raisin cookies, and it turns out adding just a splash to the cookie dough is quite delicious. A barleywine-style ale or a higher-alcohol aged barleywine can be used. Drink the rest of the barleywine with the cookies as it makes a nice dessert beer option for pairing.

MAKES ABOUT 26 COOKIES

2½ cups whole-wheat flour
½ cup old-fashioned rolled oats
1 teaspoon ground cinnamon
1 teaspoon baking powder
1 teaspoon baking soda
1 teaspoon fine sea salt
1 cup (2 sticks) unsalted butter, softened
1 cup granulated sugar
1 cup packed light brown sugar
1 large egg
1 ounce barleywine
½ cup raisins
½ cup chopped raw walnuts

Preheat the oven to 350°F. Cover a large baking sheet with parchment paper or a silicone baking mat.

Stir together the flour, oats, cinnamon, baking powder, baking soda, and salt in a medium bowl. Set aside.

Add the butter, granulated sugar, and brown sugar to the bowl of an electric mixer. Turn the mixer to medium and then medium-high. Mix until light and creamy, about 2 minutes. Scrape the sides of the bowl as needed. Mix in the egg and then the beer.

With the mixer on low, gradually add the dry ingredients. Continue to mix until all ingredients are combined into a dough. With the mixer on low, mix in the raisins and walnuts.

Roll the dough into balls about the size of a golf ball, place on the prepared baking sheet, and flatten slightly to help them spread. They are fairly large cookies so bake only 8 to a pan to allow them room to spread. Bake for 12 to 14 minutes, until the centers are firm and the edges begin to brown.

Remove from the oven. Let cool on the sheet pan for 1 to 2 minutes, then transfer to a cooling rack to cool completely. Store in an airtight container for up to 3 days.

Beers to consider: Anchor Brewing Old Foghorn Ale, Sierra Nevada Brewing Company Bigfoot Barleywine Style Ale, AleSmith Brewing Company Old Numbskull Barleywine Ale

Chocolate Pecan Coconut Porter Cake

PORTER

This cake is inspired by the traditional favorite I grew up with, German chocolate cake. A simple, single-layer cake, it is enhanced with coconut porter and topped with a caramel base that is blended into a light and fluffy frosting. Use a coconut porter if you can find one. Otherwise, choose one with coffee, chocolate, or vanilla notes.

SERVES 10 TO 12

CAKE
1½ cups cake flour
2 teaspoons baking powder
¼ cup unsweetened cocoa powder
1 cup granulated sugar
½ cup (1 stick) unsalted butter, melted and cooled
1 ounce unsweetened baking chocolate, melted and cooled
2 large eggs
6 ounces porter

Note: I prefer to use larger unsweetened coconut chips or flakes for the cake because they give a pleasant crunchy texture to each bite versus the chewy texture that is often associated with shredded coconut. Any type of unsweetened shredded coconut can be substituted if you can't find coconut chips or flakes.

Preheat the oven to 350°F. Cut a circle of parchment paper to fit a 9-inch springform pan and line the bottom of the pan with it.

Stir together the flour, baking powder, and cocoa powder in a small bowl. Set aside.

Mix together the sugar and butter in the bowl of an electric mixer for about 2 minutes, until blended and somewhat smooth. Mix in the cooled melted chocolate and then mix in the eggs.

Gradually add the dry ingredients with the mixer on low. Pour in the beer and increase the speed to medium. Scrape the sides of the bowl as needed. Mix just until all ingredients are combined, about 30 seconds.

Pour the batter into the prepared springform pan. Place the pan on a baking sheet and bake for 35 to 40 minutes, until a toothpick inserted in the center comes out clean.

Remove from the oven and let the cake cool on a cooling rack for 10 minutes. Run a knife along the edge of the cake to release the sides and then remove the sides of the pan. Let the cake cool completely.

continued

FROSTING

2 large egg yolks, beaten
½ cup packed light brown sugar
4 tablespoons (½ stick) unsalted
    butter
¼ cup whole milk
2 ounces porter
2 cups confectioners' sugar
½ cup chopped dry-roasted pecans
½ cup unsweetened coconut chips
    or flakes
¼ teaspoon fine sea salt
Pecans and coconut, for garnish

While the cake bakes, begin the frosting. Stir together the egg yolks and brown sugar in a medium saucepan. Add the butter, milk, and beer. Stir over medium heat as the mixture begins to simmer and thicken, about 12 minutes. Strain the caramel sauce through a mesh colander and into a heat-safe container to remove any solids that may have formed. Let it cool to room temperature.

Pour the caramel sauce into the bowl of an electric mixer. Add the confectioners' sugar a little at a time and then turn the mixer to medium-high. Mix until the frosting is light and fluffy. Stir in the pecans, coconut, and salt.

Frost the cooled cake and garnish with chopped pecans and coconut before slicing to serve. This cake is best served the day it's made, but leftovers can be stored in an airtight container for up to 1 day.

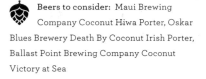 **Beers to consider:** Maui Brewing Company Coconut Hiwa Porter, Oskar Blues Brewery Death By Coconut Irish Porter, Ballast Point Brewing Company Coconut Victory at Sea

DIPA Fruit and Nut Holiday Cake

A DIPA makes an ideal substitute for more traditional bourbon and rum when soaking fruits and nuts for holiday cakes. This beer has the powerful punch of being higher in alcohol than a standard IPA, but it also lends its herbal, piney, and citrus notes from the strong hop profile. Any pleasantly pungent, hoppy DIPA is a good choice. I go my own way when making fruit cakes by selecting my favorite, familiar dried fruits and plenty of holiday spices.

MAKES 2 (8½-BY-4½-INCH) LOAVES

CAKE
1 cup dried cherries
½ cup chopped dried apricots
½ cup chopped dried pineapple
12 ounces double or imperial IPA
2½ cups unbleached all-purpose flour
1 teaspoon ground cinnamon
1 teaspoon ground nutmeg
½ teaspoon baking powder
¼ teaspoon ground clove
¼ teaspoon ground ginger
¼ teaspoon fine sea salt
Pinch of ground cardamom
1 cup chopped raw pecans
1 cup granulated sugar
¾ cup (1½ sticks) unsalted butter, softened
¼ cup light or dark molasses
3 eggs, yolks and whites separated
½ cup whole milk

Note: Plan ahead. The fruit will need to soak for at least 8 hours, and the cake should be served well chilled.

Place the cherries, apricots, and pineapple in a medium bowl. Pour in the beer. Stir to coat all of the fruit and let any foaming subside. Cover with a lid or plastic wrap and place in the refrigerator for at least 8 hours.

When you are ready to make the cake, preheat the oven to 325°F. Grease and flour two 8½-by-4½-inch loaf pans.

Stir together the flour, cinnamon, nutmeg, baking powder, clove, ginger, salt, and cardamom in a medium bowl. Toss in the pecans and set aside.

Mix together the 1 cup of sugar and softened butter in an electric mixer on medium-high until light and creamy, about 3 minutes. Mix in the molasses and then the egg yolks. Blend in the milk.

Gradually add the dry ingredients and mix on low, and then medium until a thick batter forms, about 1 minute. Scrape the sides of the bowl as needed.

Drain any excess soaking liquid from the fruit. Add the fruit to the batter, mixing until it is evenly distributed, about 30 seconds.

Use a hand mixer or separate electric mixer to beat the egg whites to soft peaks. Fold the egg whites into the cake batter by hand. Divide the batter evenly between the two loaf pans.

continued

GLAZE

⅓ cup fresh orange juice

¼ cup granulated sugar

Bake for 55 to 60 minutes, until a toothpick inserted into the center comes out clean.

While the cake bakes, stir together the orange juice and sugar in a small saucepan over medium heat until the sugar dissolves, about 5 minutes. Bring to a simmer and cook for 30 seconds. Remove from the heat.

Place the loaf pans on a cooling rack. Poke the top of the cakes in a few places with a toothpick. Evenly pour an equal amount of the orange glaze over the surface of each cake. Let cool for 30 minutes.

Run a knife along the sides of the cake in the pan. Flip each pan onto a large piece of plastic wrap to remove the cake from the pan. Wrap in plastic wrap and refrigerate until well chilled, about 4 hours, before slicing to serve. The cake will keep in the fridge for up to 5 days, or freeze for up to a month.

Beers to consider: Ninkasi Brewing Company Tricerahops Double India Pale Ale, Green Flash Brewing Company West Coast IPA, Stone Brewing Ruination Double IPA 2.0

Session IPA Pound Cake

SESSION BEER

I was several years into cooking and baking as a profession before I learned how the pound cake got its name. Simply, traditional recipes called for a pound of butter, sugar, and flour. I rarely make that much cake at one time, so by my definition a pound cake is a rich and buttery cake with hints of citrus. Those hints are made bolder by the addition of a fruity IPA. A session IPA is a good choice for this cake because session beers are lower in alcohol, and session IPAs tend to be less hoppy, which allows for the citrus notes, and not the hoppy bitterness, to shine.

SERVES 8 TO 10

1½ cups unbleached all-purpose flour

1 teaspoon baking powder

¼ teaspoon fine sea salt

1 teaspoon orange zest

½ teaspoon lemon zest

1¼ cups granulated sugar

½ cup (1 stick) unsalted butter, softened

2 large eggs

4 ounces session IPA

Preheat the oven to 350°F. Grease an 8½-by-4½-inch loaf pan with butter.

Stir together the flour, baking powder, and salt in a medium bowl. Add the orange zest and lemon zest. Set aside.

Add the sugar and butter to the bowl of an electric mixer. Mix on medium and then medium-high until light and creamy, about 2 minutes. Mix in the eggs one at a time. Scrape the sides of the bowl as needed.

Gradually add the dry ingredients with the mixer on low. Then slowly pour in the beer. Mix on medium until the ingredients form a smooth batter, about 30 seconds.

Transfer the batter to the prepared loaf pan. Bake for 46 to 48 minutes, until a toothpick inserted into the center of the pound cake comes out clean. Remove from the oven.

Set the pan on a cooling rack and let cool for 20 minutes. Run a knife along the sides of the cake. Place a serving plate over the loaf pan and invert to release the cake from the pan. Serve warm or at room temperature. Store the cake in an airtight container for up to 2 days.

Beers to consider: Firestone Walker Brewing Company Easy Jack IPA, Uinta Brewing Wyld Simcoe Session Ale, Ballast Point Brewing Company Even Keel Session IPA

Holiday Ale Cut-Out Cookies

These tender cookies use a concentrated spiced holiday ale and orange zest to create a dough that can be rolled thick and cut into all kinds of fun holiday shapes. They are perfectly enjoyable as they are, but feel free to decorate them with your favorite frosting. Choose a winter-warmer style with an IBU of less than 40 with notes of holiday spice.

MAKES 26 TO 28 COOKIES,
DEPENDING ON THE SIZE OF
COOKIE CUTTERS

BEER REDUCTION
12 ounces holiday ale
3 tablespoons light brown sugar

COOKIES
3 cups unbleached all-purpose flour
1 tablespoon orange zest
½ teaspoon fine sea salt
¼ teaspoon ground allspice
¼ teaspoon ground nutmeg
Pinch of ground black pepper
Pinch of ground clove
1 cup (2 sticks) unsalted butter,
    softened
½ cup packed light brown sugar
½ cup granulated sugar
1 large egg
1 teaspoon pure vanilla extract

Note: Plan ahead. The beer is reduced to concentrate the flavor. This process can take 30 to 45 minutes. The dough will need to rest in the fridge for an hour. Once cut, the trays will also need to sit in the freezer for 10 minutes. (It's a great trick for helping the cookies keep their shape and clean edges during baking.)

To make the reduction, stir together the beer and brown sugar in a medium saucepan. Bring to a simmer over medium-high heat, then reduce the heat to medium to maintain a heavy simmer to a very low boil. Continue to cook, stirring often, until the beer reduces to about 1½ ounces, 30 to 45 minutes. Watch the beer closely as it nears its full reduction as it can burn if not stirred often. Set aside to cool completely.

Stir together the flour, orange zest, salt, allspice, nutmeg, pepper, and clove in a medium bowl. Set aside.

Blend together the butter, ½ cup brown sugar, and granulated sugar in the bowl of an electric mixer on medium-high until light and creamy, about 3 minutes. Scrape the sides of the bowl as needed.

Mix in the egg, and then the beer reduction and vanilla. The batter may look slightly lumpy. With the mixer on low, gradually add the dry ingredients. Mix on medium until combined into a ball of dough.

continued

Divide the dough into two equal balls and transfer each to a sheet of plastic wrap. Flatten into a disk and wrap. Refrigerate for 1 hour.

Roll out each disk on a floured surface to ½ inch thickness. Cut with desired shapes. Transfer the cookies to an ungreased baking sheet, at least 1 inch apart. Place the cookie sheet in the freezer for 10 minutes. Form dough scraps back into one disk, refrigerate until you are ready to roll, cut, freeze, and bake.

Preheat the oven to 350°F. Bake the cookies for 14 minutes, until the edges are slightly browned. Remove from the oven. Let cool for 2 to 3 minutes on the baking sheet, then transfer to a cooling rack to cool completely. Cookies will keep in an airtight container for up to 4 days, or freeze for up to 1 month.

Beers to consider: Great Lakes Brewing Company Christmas Ale, Breckenridge Brewery Christmas Ale, Thirsty Dog Brewing Company 12 Dogs of Christmas Ale

Pretzel Bread Pudding

with Amber Ale Chocolate Sauce

AMBER ALE

It's not uncommon for my mom to go brewpub hopping with me when I visit my hometown. On a recent outing, we were both intrigued by a pretzel bread pudding on a dessert menu. The original didn't incorporate beer, but I knew right away that the biscuity, toffee flavors of an amber ale would send this dessert over the top. The sweeter with more toffee notes, the better.

SERVES 10 TO 12

PRETZELS

3 tablespoons granulated sugar, divided

½ cup water, heated to 110 to 115°F

1 tablespoon active dry yeast

4 cups unbleached all-purpose flour

6 ounces amber ale

6 tablespoons (¾ stick) unsalted butter, melted and cooled, divided

½ teaspoon ground cinnamon, divided

½ teaspoon fine sea salt

Cooking oil or butter to grease the bowl

3 quarts water

⅓ cup baking soda

Note: This recipe uses homemade sweet beer pretzels, and it's best to make them the day before you make the bread pudding. If you aren't feeling ambitious, you can substitute sweet store-bought pretzels. When you aren't in the mood for bread pudding, you might also consider making the pretzel sticks and chocolate sauce, and stopping right there. It makes an equally satisfying treat.

Begin by making the pretzels. Stir 2 tablespoons of the sugar into the warm water. Stir in the yeast. Let sit until it blooms, about 5 minutes. Add the flour to the bowl of an electric mixer fitted with the dough hook. With mixer on low, pour in the bloomed yeast.

Mix in the beer, followed by 5 tablespoons of the melted butter, ¼ teaspoon of the cinnamon, and the salt. Let the mixer knead the dough until it forms a ball in the center of the bowl. Continue to mix about 2 more minutes. Turn the dough out onto a floured surface and knead by hand for another 2 to 3 minutes, until smooth and elastic. Form the dough into a ball. Grease the bottom and sides of a large bowl with cooking oil. Place the dough ball in the bowl, cover with a clean dish towel, and let sit in a draft-free area to rise until doubled in size, about 1 hour.

Punch down the dough and form into a ball. Cut into 16 equal pieces. Roll each piece into a cord about 7 inches long. Twist two cords together and tuck under the ends. This will make 8 pretzel sticks.

Preheat the oven to 425°F. Bring the water and baking soda to a boil in a large soup pot. Work one to two at a time and, carefully, drop the pretzel

continued

BREAD PUDDING

8 day-old pretzel twists, cubed
(about 12 cups)
4 cups whole milk
½ cup granulated sugar
4 tablespoons (½ stick) unsalted
butter
4 large eggs, beaten
1 teaspoon pure vanilla extract
¼ teaspoon ground cinnamon
¼ teaspoon fine sea salt

CHOCOLATE SAUCE

1 cup granulated sugar
¾ cup unsweetened cocoa
½ cup whole milk
4 tablespoons (½ stick) unsalted
butter
2 ounces amber ale
Pinch of fine sea salt
Vanilla ice cream, for serving
(optional)

sticks into the boiling water. Cook until they float to the top, 30 to 60 seconds. Use a slotted spoon to transfer each stick to a baking sheet covered in parchment paper or a silicone mat, about 4 per baking sheet.

Brush each pretzel with some of the remaining 1 tablespoon of melted butter. Stir together the remaining ¼ teaspoon of cinnamon and 1 tablespoon of sugar in a small bowl. Sprinkle each pretzel stick generously with cinnamon sugar. Bake for 15 minutes, until dark golden brown.

To make the bread pudding, preheat the oven to 350°F. Spray a 9-by-13-inch baking dish with nonstick cooking spray or coat with butter. Spread the cubes of pretzel in a single layer in the dish.

Stir together the milk, ½ cup sugar, and 4 tablespoons butter in a medium saucepan over medium heat until the butter is melted. Let cool for 15 minutes. Whisk together the eggs in a small bowl. Add about ¼ cup of the cool liquid to the eggs and whisk. Next, whisk the egg mixture into the liquid to blend well. Stir in the vanilla, ¼ teaspoon cinnamon, and ¼ teaspoon salt.

Pour the liquid over the pretzels. Gently press with a spatula so that the bread soaks it up. Place the baking dish on a large baking sheet to catch any potential boil-overs. Bake for 40 to 45 minutes, until the top and edges are golden brown and the center is firm. Let cool while you make the chocolate sauce.

Stir all the sauce ingredients in a medium saucepan over medium heat to melt the butter. Let it come to a boil over medium heat and boil for 1 minute. Remove from the heat and allow to cool for 10 to 15 minutes.

To serve, place a scoop of warm bread pudding in a bowl and drizzle with chocolate sauce. Top with a scoop of vanilla ice cream, if desired.

Vanilla Porter Pecan and Walnut Pie

PORTER

I enjoy a classic pecan pie, but over the years I've adapted this traditional holiday dessert. I like to add chopped nuts versus halves, and there is no harm in going beyond pecans by adding a few walnuts. A splash of porter in both the crust and filling balances the sweetness with slightly bitter, roasted notes. Any porter will work, but one with vanilla, chocolate, or coffee notes is even better.

SERVES 8

CRUST
1 cup unbleached all-purpose flour
1 tablespoon granulated sugar
½ teaspoon fine sea salt
½ cup (1 stick) cold unsalted butter, cubed
1½ ounces porter, chilled

FILLING
1 cup packed light brown sugar
6 tablespoons (¾ stick) unsalted butter, cubed
¼ cup light corn syrup
1 ounce porter
¼ teaspoon fine sea salt
3 large eggs
1 cup chopped raw pecans
½ cup chopped raw walnuts

Preheat the oven to 350°F.

Make the crust by placing the flour, sugar, and salt in a food processor. Add the butter and pulse in 10-second intervals until it is chopped into pea-sized pieces. Pour in the beer and process on low until the dough comes together in a ball. Wrap the dough ball in plastic wrap and refrigerate for 15 minutes.

Make the filling while the dough rests. Stir together the brown sugar, butter, corn syrup, and porter in a medium saucepan over medium heat, until all ingredients are melted together, about 5 minutes. Stir in the salt. Let cool completely.

Beat the eggs gently in a medium bowl to break up the yolks. Pour the cooled melted sugars and butter into the bowl and stir to combine. Fold in the pecans and walnuts. Set aside.

Roll the dough on a floured surface to make about a 12-inch circle. Transfer the dough to a deep 9-inch pie pan. Gently press the dough into the pan and crimp the edges. Place the pie pan on a baking sheet. Pour the filling into the crust.

Bake for 55 to 60 minutes, until the top is browned and the center no longer jiggles when you move the pie. Remove from the oven and let cool for at least 10 minutes before serving. Serve warm or at room temperature.

Beers to consider: Breckenridge Brewery Vanilla Porter, Rogue Ales Mocha Porter, Hangar 24 Craft Brewery Chocolate Bomber Porter

Scottish Ale Shortbread Squares

SCOTTISH ALE

Shortbread is something that I thought could not get any better. But adding a splash of good Scottish ale proved me wrong. Scottish ales are typically low in hoppiness but heavy on malt and caramelized flavors. These are qualities that bring out the best in buttery shortbread. A higher-alcohol Scotch ale is also fine to use. Scottish ale goes well with this shortbread as a dessert pairing, too. But don't overlook a good coffee-infused stout or chocolate porter.

MAKES 25 SQUARES

¾ cup (1½ sticks) unsalted butter, softened
½ cup confectioners' sugar
¼ cup packed dark brown sugar
¼ teaspoon fine sea salt
1 ounce Scottish ale
2 cups unbleached, all-purpose flour

Preheat the oven to 325°F. Grease an 8-inch square baking pan with butter.

Add the butter and confectioners' sugar to the bowl of an electric mixer. Mix on medium and then medium-high until it becomes light and creamy, about 2 minutes. Add the brown sugar, and cream for 1 more minute. Add the salt. Scrape the sides of the bowl as needed.

Pour in the beer and mix on medium until blended in, about 30 seconds. Gradually add the flour a little at a time with the mixer on low. Increase the speed to medium and mix until a dough forms.

Transfer the cookie dough to the prepared pan and press it into an even layer. Bake for 45 minutes, or until the edges are browned and the center is firm. Remove from the oven.

Let cool for 5 minutes, and then use a knife to cut the shortbread into 25 squares while it is still warm. Let cool completely before serving. Store in an airtight container for up to 3 days.

Beers to consider: Ballast Point Brewing Company Piper Down Scottish Ale, Founders Brewing Company Dirty Bastard Scotch Ale, Oskar Blues Brewery Old Chub Scotch Ale

Saison Black Pepper Brownies

SAISON OR FARMHOUSE ALE

A savory spice in a chocolate dessert adds a hint of an unusual, yet addicting, flavor that makes you curious about the secret ingredient. These brownies have two: black pepper and saison. The light, peppery notes of the saison is a perfect match for black pepper. Both come together with the chocolate to create a one-of-a-kind brownie. Stick with a classic saison versus a specially hopped or aged version.

SERVES 9

½ cup (1 stick) unsalted butter, plus more for greasing
1 ounce unsweetened baking chocolate
¼ cup unsweetened cocoa powder
1 cup granulated sugar
2 large eggs
1½ ounces saison
½ cup unbleached all-purpose flour
½ teaspoon baking powder
½ teaspoon fine sea salt
½ teaspoon ground black pepper, plus a pinch for topping
2 tablespoons confectioners' sugar

Preheat the oven to 350°F. Grease an 8-inch square baking pan with butter.

Melt the butter and unsweetened chocolate together in a saucepan over medium-low heat, 5 to 7 minutes. Stir often. Remove the pan from the heat and whisk in the cocoa powder.

Transfer the butter and chocolate to a medium mixing bowl. Stir in the granulated sugar, and allow it to cool until it's just barely warm, about 10 minutes. Stir in the eggs. Pour in the beer and stir until mixed into the batter. Set aside.

Toss together the flour, baking powder, salt, and ½ teaspoon of pepper in a small bowl. Gradually add the dry ingredients to the chocolate. Stir just until combined.

Pour the batter into the prepared baking pan and bake 20 to 23 minutes, until a fork inserted in the center comes out clean. Let the brownies cool for 15 to 20 minutes.

Stir together the confectioners' sugar and pinch of pepper. Use a small hand strainer to dust the brownies with confectioners' sugar until covered. Cut into 9 brownies and remove from the pan. Dust with any remaining sugar, if desired. Store brownies in an airtight container up to 3 days.

 Beers to consider: North Coast Brewing Company Le Merle, Firestone Walker Brewing Company Opal, 21st Amendment Brewery Sneak Attack Saison

Milk Stout Caramel Tart

STOUT

With a thick layer of soft, slightly chewy salted caramel over a sugar cookie crust, this dessert is downright dreamy. A little creamy milk stout added to the caramel deepens the flavor and lends a subtle bite of pleasant bitterness that is a perfect match for the sweet and salty caramel. A sweet or milk stout is ideal, but avoid heavy coffee notes for this one.

SERVES 10 TO 12

CRUST
½ cup (1 stick) unsalted butter, softened
½ cup granulated sugar
1 large egg
1 teaspoon pure vanilla extract
¼ teaspoon fine sea salt
1¾ cups unbleached all-purpose flour

Note: You will need to bake the tart crust before adding the caramel filling. If you don't have pie weights for the blind baking (prebaking), about 2 cups of dried beans will do the job.

To make the crust, mix together ½ cup of the butter and ½ cup of sugar until light and creamy, about 3 minutes on medium-high. Mix in the egg. Scrape the sides of the bowl as needed.

With the mixer on low, add the vanilla and the salt. Gradually add the flour and increase the speed to medium. Mix until a cookie dough comes together, 1 to 2 minutes.

Preheat the oven to 375°F.

Transfer the dough to a 10-inch fluted tart pan with a removable bottom. Press the dough evenly into the tart pan, spreading it up along the sides to fill the pan. Prick the dough in several places with a fork and place in the freezer for 10 minutes.

Cover the tart crust with foil. Fill with pie weights or dried beans. Bake for 25 minutes, until golden brown. Remove from the oven. Once the foil is cool you can remove and discard it. Let the crust cool completely.

continued

FILLING

1 cup heavy cream
1 cup packed light brown sugar
¾ cup light corn syrup
½ cup (1 stick) unsalted butter
½ cup granulated sugar
½ teaspoon fine sea salt
4 ounces stout
1 teaspoon pure vanilla extract
Flaked sea salt, for garnish

To make the caramel, cook the cream, brown sugar, corn syrup, butter, granulated sugar, and salt in a medium heavy saucepan over medium heat, stirring constantly, until the sugar is dissolved and the butter is melted, about 5 minutes.

Remove the pan from the heat and stir in the beer. Return to medium heat and insert a candy thermometer. From this point forward, do not stir. Allow the caramel to come to a boil. Watch it closely as the beer will foam a bit in the beginning. Reduce the heat to medium-low if necessary. Cook to 240°F. This can take 30 to 45 minutes.

Remove the caramel from the heat. Stir in the vanilla. Carefully pour the hot caramel into the cooled crust. Let cool until firm enough to slice, about 1 hour. Just before serving sprinkle with flaked sea salt.

Beers to consider: Odell Brewing Company Lugene Chocolate Milk Stout, Left Hand Brewing Company Milk Stout, Belching Beaver Brewery Beavers Milk Stout

Blackberry Ale Hand Pies

Fruit ales add sweetness and depth to fruity desserts. There is no need to stick with blackberry beer. Another berry beer, or even a peach or apricot beer, adds a nice touch. I always find that hand pies are a fun way to switch things up and keep dessert interesting. Serve these with fruit ale on the side. A little vanilla ice cream won't hurt, either.

MAKES 12 PIES

CRUST
2 cups unbleached all-purpose flour
1 tablespoon of granulated sugar
½ teaspoon fine sea salt
1 cup (2 sticks) cold unsalted butter, cubed
1 teaspoon fruit ale, chilled
¼ cup ice cold water

FILLING
½ cup granulated sugar
3 tablespoons cornstarch
1 ounce fruit ale
2 cups blackberries (about 10 ounces)
Pinch of fine ground sea salt

Note: Plan ahead. The crust will need to rest in the fridge for about 20 minutes before you can make the pies.

For the crust, place the flour, sugar, and salt in the bowl of a food processor. Add the butter and pulse for 5- to 10-second intervals until the butter is finely chopped into pea-sized pieces and evenly distributed. With the processor on low, add 1 teaspoon of the beer, and then pour in the water 1 tablespoon at a time, until the dough comes together into a ball. It should be fairly firm and not sticky.

Wrap the ball of dough in plastic wrap and let rest in the fridge for 20 minutes.

For the filling, stir together the sugar, cornstarch, 1 ounce of the beer, blackberries, and salt in a medium bowl.

Preheat the oven to 350°F.

Cut the dough in half. Return one half to the refrigerator. Roll the other half to ¼ inch thickness on a lightly floured surface. Cut the dough into six, 4½-inch circles. You will likely need to reroll the dough to get all six.

Place the six circles of dough on a large baking sheet covered in parchment paper or a silicone mat. Place a generous tablespoon of filling in the center of each circle, about 3 to 4 berries, and a teaspoon of juices.

continued

EGG WASH

1 large egg

1 tablespoon water

GLAZE

½ cup confectioners' sugar, sifted

½ ounce fruit ale

Pinch of fine sea salt

Whisk together the egg and water. Brush around the edges of each circle with egg wash. Fold the dough in half to create a half-moon. Pinch the two ends of the dough together. Bake until some of the juices are visible and bubbling, and the edges of the pies begin to brown, about 25 minutes. Repeat with the remaining dough and filling.

Transfer the pies to a cooling rack to cool completely.

For the glaze, stir together the confectioners' sugar, ½ ounce of the beer, and salt until smooth. Drizzle each pie with the glaze. Let the glaze set for 5 to 10 minutes and serve.

Beers to consider: Founders Brewing Company Rubaeus, Boston Beer Company Samuel Adams Blackberry Witbier, Sea Dog Brewing Company Blueberry Wheat Ale

ACKNOWLEDGMENTS

A special thanks to my agent, Leslie Stoker, my editor, Ann Treistman, and the hard-working team at Countryman Press. To Jane Bonacci without whom the idea for this book would have always been on my back burner. Thanks to my second set of eyes for so many photos, Tracey Hagan. I'm grateful to all my friends—chefs, recipe developers, food bloggers, beer lovers, and home cooks—who graciously helped test recipes. Thanks to my parents and the rest of my family who have eagerly been awaiting publication. Finally, thanks to my best friend and brewery touring partner, my husband, Dan, for fielding brewing questions, eating beer-infused food for months on end, and always nudging me to take advantage of opportunities.

INDEX